THE
CHRISTMAS TREE
BOOK

The Step-by-Step Guide to Buying and Decorating Your Tree
with Lighting, Ornaments, Ribbons, and More!

CASSIE KITZMILLER

Skyhorse Publishing

Skyhorse Publishing books may be purchased in bulk at special discounts for sales promotion, corporate gifts, fund-raising, or educational purposes. Special editions can also be created to specifications. For details, contact the Special Sales Department, Skyhorse Publishing, 307 West 36th Street, 11th Floor, New York, NY 10018 or info@skyhorsepublishing.com.

Skyhorse® and Skyhorse Publishing® are registered trademarks of Skyhorse Publishing, Inc.®, a Delaware corporation.

Visit our website at www.skyhorsepublishing.com.

10 9 8 7 6 5 4 3 2 1

Library of Congress Cataloging-in-Publication Data is available on file.

Cover design by Mona Lin
Cover photographs by RAZ Imports

Print ISBN: 978-1-5107-5210-8
Ebook ISBN: 978-1-5107-5211-5

Printed in China

Contents

Let's Get Decorating

Welcome to *The Christmas Tree Book!* I am so excited that you have decided to join me on a journey to designing your best-looking Christmas tree ever! If you are reading this, it is safe to assume that you love all things Christmas, and you are in good company. Christmas is a magical season where friends, family, and loved ones gather to share old stories and make new memories around the very special heart of the holiday home—the Christmas tree. My hope is for this book to become a reference tool that you can come back to time and time again as you decorate your own Christmas tree through the years.

Throughout the book, I compare designing your tree to creating a beautiful piece of art. Just as a beautiful piece of art can anchor a room and add life and beauty to a space, a Christmas tree adds a special kind of magic to any room it graces. This book will walk you through the materials and techniques needed to bring your masterpiece to fruition. Just as there are a million different styles of art and many different creation techniques, there are also many different styles of Christmas trees and endless decorating techniques.

There is truly no wrong way to decorate a beautiful tree, and I trust that you will be able to find tips and techniques in this book that will inspire you to design your best-looking tree yet. So, whether you like a tree loaded with gilt and glitter from top to bottom or you like a simpler tree featuring special family ornaments, I encourage you to grab your copy of the ***Custom Christmas Tree-Decorating Checklist*** located in the back of this book and online at: www.findingbeautyintheeveryday.com/checklist, grab a big mug of hot cocoa, and get to planning your best-looking Christmas tree ever!

1 | Introducing Your Personal Tree-Decorating Elf

*"I will honor Christmas in my heart,
and try to keep it all the year."*
—Charles Dickens from *A Christmas Carol*

The Christmas season is truly the most magical time of the year, and I am here to guide you through the tips and techniques required to decorate the star of your Holiday home, the Christmas tree. So many of our Holiday festivities, favorite memories, and special times are centered around the Christmas tree, and as such, it should be given the "royal treatment" it deserves!

If you are looking for a "One-Stop Shop" on decorating a beautiful, designer-quality Christmas tree, then you have come to the right place! In the following chapters, I will guide you step by step through selecting your design, choosing a tree, maximizing your lights, and planning the exact steps and materials you need to create a custom, one-of-a-kind Christmas tree.

With the skills you gain from this book, you will be able to decorate your tree faster and with greater ease, and your end results will have your friends and family saying, "Wow!"

Before I get into all of the tips and techniques that you will implement to create your best Christmas tree ever, let me introduce myself.

My name is Cassie and I will be your personal "Tree-Decorating Elf" throughout this book. At only five feet tall, and with over ten years of professional Christmas

tree-decorating experience, I am just grateful that I don't have pointy ears or people may really start to wonder!

I started in the Christmas business while I was still in college, majoring in Interior Design. I marched into our local design store and boldly asked for a job with no prior design experience and little education under my belt. My mentor and fellow business partner, Marty, took a risk and hired me for my first "Design" job, which was exceptionally glamorous—unpacking boxes in the stock room and cleaning the store.

From those humble beginnings I worked my way into other positions in the store and soon began helping decorate the Christmas trees during the busy Holiday season. Something clicked for me while I was decorating the trees, and I really began to throw myself into the process of designing beautiful trees with unique elements and features.

Customers soon requested my help in designing trees in their own homes with my unique touches and ideas. This experience really fueled my creativity and clarified the many styles and personalities available in the Christmas tree market. During this time, I was also attending Buyer's Markets twice a year and taking classes from some of the top designers in the field in order to continue to hone my skills and gain new ideas.

Fast-forward a couple years, and I was given the opportunity to join with other like-minded business women, opening a year-round Christmas store! My role in the new store was tree design, and I was able to decorate, sell, and then redecorate Christmas trees all day long, all year long! I was in Christmas heaven! The Christmas store opened the door to more decorating clients, and I found myself decorating Christmas trees nonstop, from the middle of October through the middle of December.

I have now been decorating Christmas trees for over ten years and for hundreds of clients. During this journey I have picked up some valuable skills and techniques that make decorating a beautiful Christmas tree fast and easy, and the results are truly one-of-a-kind.

Several times a season, I have the opportunity to teach decorating classes on tree design. After class, I am always approached by people thanking me for the information, and they always say the same thing: "I never knew there was so much to learn about decorating my tree!" That is the motivation for this book, to help others learn the ins and outs of decorating a beautiful tree for themselves and their families.

Let's Get Started: Stay organized and keep track of your ideas by grabbing your copy of the Tree-Decorating Checklist now!

Throughout this book I will share with you the secrets to Christmas Tree-Decorating success. I will give you step-by step instructions on how to decorate your tree, as well as, the materials necessary to create your Dream Tree. I have also included a **Custom Christmas Tree-Decorating Checklist** in the back of the book. I encourage you to use it to guide you on your Tree-Decorating journey.

Decorating a beautiful Christmas tree is truly creating a piece of art. A well-decorated Christmas tree results in a three-dimensional art form that your family can enjoy for the entire Holiday season. Just as an artist must gather the correct supplies and execute special techniques in order to create a beautifully finished design, so it is with decorating a beautiful tree; you need to utilize the correct materials and techniques to complete your tree design. This book is your guide for creating a Christmas tree that will have your friends and family asking, "Did YOU really decorate that?!"

In the following chapters, I am going to walk you through every step of your tree-decorating journey. To kick things off, we are going to dig into selecting your design style or theme. Then we are going to discuss how to select your perfect tree as well as some simple tips to add that extra wow factor through your lighting. We will then jump into the materials needed to create your design, and I will walk you through the correct order of application to ensure that your tree is full and lush, without looking cluttered and messy.

In the following chapters, we are going to walk through every step of the tree-decorating journey. Together, we are going to cover:

- Selecting a design style or theme.
- Choosing the perfect tree and whether to go with real or artificial.
- Lighting tips, techniques, and trade tricks for extra "wow" factor.
- Necessary materials and products to complete your look.
- The exact order to apply your decorations to your tree in order to save you time, energy, and your sanity!
- Coordinating your topper and tree base for a cohesive overall design.

The "extra-special" little touches that will make your tree really shine!

Along the way, you are going to learn some "Trade Secrets" that will give you the designer look that you long for and will allow your tree to take center stage this Holiday season. I will also include some practical tips to use many of your existing decorations in new ways so you can utilize your favorite pieces from Christmases past.

In the next chapter, we will uncover the importance of clarifying your end goal and discuss the difference between a tree style and a tree theme. Now let's stop chit chatting and get going!

"One of the most glorious messes in the world is the mess created in the living room on Christmas Day."

-Andy Rooney

2 | Defining Your Look

Now that you know a little about me, and how we are going to approach decorating our tree, it is time to get started! However, before you hang your first ornament, it is essential to begin this process by thinking about your end goal. What do you want your Christmas tree to look like when you are finished? When you have an end look or vision in place it guides all of your decisions moving forward in order to get the finished product you desire!

In this chapter, we are going to focus on clarifying the finished look for your tree. This will allow you to select the materials and techniques that will make your tree uniquely yours! So, where to begin?

Very few sculptors begin their process by sitting down at the table and taking random hacks at a chunk of marble. That would be ridiculous and a waste of perfectly good time and materials. The same is true if you begin your design process by randomly buying decorations and hanging them on your tree. The best designs begin with a plan in mind, and you need to start by researching and brainstorming what style or theme you want for your Christmas tree.

Designer Tip: You get the best finished product when you start with the end goal in mind!

You may be wondering the about difference between a Christmas tree theme and a Christmas tree style. Well, it can be a little bit confusing, so let's break it down. A theme is usually one or two elements used together to create a unified whole.

Some examples of commonly used Christmas tree themes:

- Santas
- Snowmen
- Angels
- School Teams
- Gingerbread
- Toys
- Hobbies (such as baking, knitting, gardening, and hunting)

Themes can also be color combinations such as red and green, gold and ivory, or even magenta and lime. Any color combination can be enough to get you started on your theme. If you are considering adding a new tree to your home this year, a hobby-based themed tree is a fun option. Hobby-based themes are popular choices for decorating smaller trees in rooms such as kitchens, bedrooms, and "man caves." Gardening, baking, knitting, hunting, skiing, and an endless list of other hobbies make for fun and memorable tree themes. Animal themes are often popular, as I have decorated many bird-themed trees over the years and even one memorable cat-themed tree with over 1,000 cat ornaments and a star topper with a little mouse dangling off of a string!

Tree Theme vs. Tree Style: "A tree theme is one or two elements repeated over and over throughout the tree. A tree style is a cohesive feeling or look that utilizes many different types of materials to create a unified whole."

As a designer, I have the privilege of attending the largest Holiday Market on the East Coast every year, where I have seen some pretty wild themes. Envision one tree with chandeliers of all shapes and sizes wired into the branches and shining brightly. Another tree was decorated with holiday elves climbing the tree trying to get to a wine glass topper at the tippy top of the tree. One very memorable tree even had an Amazon animal theme complete with snake skin garlands! No matter what you like to collect or showcase during the holidays, you can turn it into a Christmas tree theme. The sky, or the top of your tree, is the limit!

Christmas tree styles are different from themes in that they use a variety of different elements to create an overall, unified feel or look.

Some popular Christmas tree styles include:

- Traditional Elegance
- Winter Wonderland
- Candy Land
- Rustic Lodge
- Vintage Victorian
- Romantic Garden
- Modern/Retro
- Farmhouse/Country

Tree styles use a variety of different products to create an overall feeling or design, as opposed to a theme, where one or two common elements are repeated over and over to achieve the desired look.

Sanity Saver: Make shopping fun and stress-free by getting clear on your vision and then focusing on those key items that will help carry out your desired theme or style.

Why is this distinction important in moving forward with your Christmas tree project? Well, if you have a vision of your goal tree in mind, clarifying your theme or style will guide you on which materials to invest in to get the finished product you desire. For example, if you are going for a rustic lodge look, but purchase only bear ornaments, you have actually produced a bear-themed tree, not the rustic lodge look you desired. You will have spent money that could have been invested in smarter places, and you will be disappointed with your end result.

So, now is the time to get out your pen and paper and your favorite research materials (magazines, Pinterest, blog posts, books, etc.) and start brainstorming your tree-decorating goals. If you are really motivated, you can even create a vision board complete with samples of trees you like, elements you want to utilize, and colors that complement your décor.

If you are having a hard time deciding on your look or even narrowing down your choices (so many tree ideas, so little time!), there are a few tips that I can offer. First, consider the location of the tree in your home, office, or venue.

What is the style of the room? If your tree sits in the middle of a large window in the center of a Victorian home, a contemporary silver-and-black tree would feel out of place. The location of the

tree could inspire you to choose a soft, vintage theme complete with nostalgic ornaments, nosegays, and clip-on candles. Think about where your tree is going to sit and brainstorm color stories, styles, or themes that would make your tree really complement its surroundings.

Another tip to gain clarity is to take a field trip to a local hotspot for ideas and inspiration. I am lucky enough to be located within an easy drive to the Biltmore Estate—a beautiful and historic mansion built by George Vanderbilt in 1895 and now a very popular tourist destination. This château-style mansion is the largest privately owned home in the United States and never fails to inspire.

Every year, Biltmore employs a team to come in and make over the estate for Christmas. There is no shortage of inspiration when you walk the floors, as trees are everywhere and all have been decorated with great skill! Think about popular destinations in your own town that may have beautiful trees and plan a trip for inspiration. Places to consider include museums, high-end hotels and resorts, charity events that host a "Festival of Trees," and popular tourist areas.

Once you have decided on a look, it is time to get out your ***Custom Christmas Tree-Decorating Checklist*** and get to decorating! In the next chapter, we learn about the different tools/materials and techniques that you will need in order to create your best Christmas tree yet!

"I never thought it was such a bad little tree. It's not bad at all, really. Maybe it just needs a little love."

-Linus van Pelt

3 | Tools and Techniques

Once you have clarified your desired look, it is time to learn about the tools and techniques necessary to create your dream tree. When I was in school for Interior Design, my course requirements included the class Drawing Fundamentals. Now, I can decorate trees all day long, but hand me a pencil and paper, and I freeze. Since it was a fundamentals class, I was not too worried though, and I headed into class ready to learn.

Let me just say, I was somehow placed in the "Advanced" fundamentals class. Every other student in the class was an Art major and had completed several years of art classes. Due to having (mostly) advanced students, our teacher decided to jump into more complex techniques, and I was left drowning in the deep end. I squeezed through the class and managed to improve a little along the way, but I learned how important it is to really learn the foundational skills and techniques before tackling a new project.

The best way to start your tree decorating is by gathering your materials. Just as an artist would not sit down to paint without a canvas, brushes, paint, and so on, you don't want to start your design without all of the correct materials in place. So, which materials do you need in order to create a fabulous finished tree?

Well, depending on your look, you will need:

- A tree
- Lights
- Garlands
- Ribbon and/or bows
- Floral or greenery stems
- Decorative filler pieces

- Ornaments in different shapes and sizes
- Topper elements
- Coordinated base items

As you can see, there are a lot of components that go into making a truly beautiful tree! In the following chapters, we are going to break down the different components and talk about where and how to use them, but for now I want to leave you with some advice when it comes to collecting your materials.

The first tip is to buy your materials (ribbon, ornaments, picks, etc.) early. There is nothing more aggravating than having the perfect tree design in your mind and arriving at the store the week after Thanksgiving to find that some of the key pieces you need to create your look are sold out. This happens more often than you would think, as your local store has to order this year's Christmas products the prior January. And by the time the holidays are here, there is no way to get additional merchandise.

Wholesalers used to backstock popular items in order to fill late requests, but with the ever-changing market and minimal overhead, that is not the case anymore. Most of your retailers are going to get the vast majority of their stock delivered and set up by mid-to-late October, so if you want the best selection, plan to do the majority of your purchasing by mid-November. Additionally, if you are looking for a particular item or a popular style, be sure to shop early so you are not disappointed!

Designer Tip: Be sure to shop early and buy extra when you are picking out your favorite items. This will save you time and money in the long run!

The second tip goes along with the first but can be even more frustrating if not heeded. My word of wisdom to you is to purchase enough items the first time around. Do not make the mistake of underestimating the quantity of items that you need to complete your look and find that your item is sold out when you go to buy more.

You can always substitute another item, but the finished look will not be as complete if you have to mix and match too many items. This is another area where your *Custom Christmas Tree-Decorating Checklist* comes in handy. I have compiled all of the different materials that you may use on your tree and listed the recommended number of items you will need for each. Once you have

completed your checklist, it is time to go shopping. (I recommend reading through the book first, before filling out your checklist.)

> **Quick tip:** Before you head out to the store, shop your existing Christmas stash first. I'm guessing that if you are reading a book on Christmas tree decorating, you probably already have a pretty good stash of decorations!

When shopping your existing decor, lay out your items by the categories listed in the book and give them a thorough evaluation. Questions you want to ask when looking over your pieces: Does this fit my style or theme for this particular tree? Is the item in good condition? (Look for fading flowers, chipped ornaments, dated items, or things you just do not like.) If the answer is *No*, toss the item in a donation box to bless someone else. You would be surprised how many women's shelters, children's homes, and other types of charities really appreciate holiday decoration donations, as their budgets rarely have room for such expenditures!

Now that you have a solid inventory of the items that you already own, it is time to make a shopping list for the items that you need to purchase and set your budget. Decorations for your tree can add up quickly, so don't feel badly if you cannot purchase everything the first year. I often advise my clients to invest in the highest-quality items that they can afford over the course of three years to complete their look. This advice allows them to be able to get the look they want without breaking the bank. Investing in your tree over the course of a few years also keeps your look new and exciting every year!

When you go shopping, I really encourage you to start with your local, independent Christmas, seasonal, or gift stores. While you may pay a little bit more for the individual items, the quality you will receive, as well as the knowledge and help you will get from the staff, will be well worth the additional money.

Think about it this way; if you purchase an ornament for $3 and you can only use it for two years because it falls apart, looks worn out, or you just get tired of it, you have invested $1.50 per season for a subpar item. On the other hand, if you invest in a beautiful ornament from your local holiday store that is priced at $9.95 and you use it for the next ten years because you love it, you have only spent $1 per season for that piece, and you have enjoyed it so much more! You are more likely to donate or hand down a quality piece, so even when you tire of the nicer ornament, your initial investment keeps on blessing others!

I know some of my favorite ornaments on my own tree are the ones passed down from my mother and grandmothers. The cost for those kinds of ornaments is truly priceless. So, the moral of this story is to shop quality, not quantity, for your tree!

If you are on a limited budget, or you are decorating a themed tree that you only plan on using for a few seasons or events, there are some places you can cut costs. Shop the big box stores for your solid colored ball ornaments. Most retailers offer boxed options for very reasonable prices, and these sets are a great way to add color to your tree for very little cost. Another way to save some dollars is to purchase boxed kits from higher-end retailers during their end-of-season sales. You can often pick up some very nice sets for 50 percent off or more. This is a wonderful way to save some money while purchasing quality pieces. Keep your eyes open for good deals and remember to purchase enough when you find the sales!

Designer Tip: Ribbon is one item where you really do get what you pay for. A quality ribbon will be able to be used season after season, while a lower-quality ribbon will have to be replaced every year, so shop wisely!

Now that you have inventoried your materials, established your reusable items, and purchased the rest, it is time to focus on the techniques needed to actually put all of these different items together into a pleasing whole.

Anyone can tell you what you need to put on your tree to make it look great, but if you get home and just start sticking things on the tree, it is going to look "okay" at best. Having a step-by-step process that you can follow will ensure your success and have you decorating the tree of your dreams in no time!

Remember my challenges in my Drawing Fundamentals class? If I had had someone to teach me the basics of drawing during the early stages, I would have saved myself so much time, frustration,

and do-overs along the way! Let me be your guide in the materials and techniques needed to decorate a beautiful tree, and you will soon have a finished design you will be proud to show off!

The following chapters will cover the individual materials in more depth as well as discuss how to apply each material correctly to achieve the best results. These steps will allow you to achieve your best-looking tree ever, with no time-consuming or costly redos. Just like a skilled baker combines the right ingredients in the correct order to create a delicious cake, you need to combine the right elements in the correct order to design a beautiful tree. Consider the following chapters your "Recipe for Success" in decorating your tree. Follow the steps in the correct order with the right ingredients, and you can't fail in creating a beautiful, magazine cover-worthy tree!

Up next, we are going to start our "Recipe for Success" with a no-fail guide to selecting the foundation of your design, the tree.

4 | Selecting Your Tree

By now you should have grabbed your copy of the *Custom Christmas Tree-Decorating Checklist,* and are ready to start decorating your tree. Yahoo!

Like any good artist, we need to start our design off with a blank canvas. In this case, our blank canvas is the actual Christmas tree itself. The look and type of your tree will greatly affect the finished product, so we are going to take a few minutes to break down the different types of trees and how to decide which is best for you and your home.

The first decision you need to make regarding on which tree is best for your design is whether you are going to use a real or artificial tree. There are pros and cons to each that will help guide your decision.

Real trees come in a variety of types depending on your location and what is available at your local nursery or tree stand. In the Blue Ridge Mountains, where I am located, we are lucky enough to have easy access to endless Fraser Firs, also known as "America's Most Popular Tree." Fraser Firs smell amazing and have strong, sturdy branches for decorating.

If you are on the West Coast, you will most likely have access to the Noble Fir, which has a growth pattern and needles similar to the Fraser Fir, but with a slight bluish cast. My Northeastern readers will have access to the Balsam Fir, which is known for its long-lasting fragrance and long-term needle retention.

There are several other styles of real trees available, including White Pine, Blue Spruce, and Norway Spruce. For anyone looking to purchase a real tree, I recommend contacting your local dealer and researching the varieties they offer before you show up to the lot ready to purchase. Each tree variety has its own personality and style, and it's important to purchase a tree that will hold up to the expectations you have for the finished product.

Come Prepared: Take some time to research your tree selections before you head to the lot. Purchasing the wrong type of tree for your needs could result in expensive broken ornaments or an undesirable result!

I personally use a real tree in my own home every year because I love the smell and look of it. To me, there is nothing like having a real tree in my home from the day after Thanksgiving to the day after Christmas. However, there are some cons to real trees that you need to consider before making your decision.

Tree allergies are not uncommon and can trigger attacks to those who are sensitive. Real trees also require a commitment to being watered regularly (twice a day in the first few days and then once a day after the first week), so if you are going to be traveling frequently, or are particularly forgetful, you may want to go with an artificial option.

Real trees are also notoriously messy. There are all kinds of tricks and tools to reduce the sap and needles, but there will always be some needles that escape. If you have new carpet, or are very particular about mess, you may be better off with an artificial tree.

Designer Tip: Real trees change their shape throughout the holiday season due to the weight of the ornaments pulling down their branches. To keep your tree looking its best, be sure to move lights, garlands, and ornaments around as needed.

Real trees are limited to the amount of weight from decorations that their branches can reasonably withstand. Different varieties of trees hold up better than others against more weight (see my fully-decorated Frasier Fir picture at the start of the chapter), but all trees will begin to droop and lower their branches throughout the season. I personally enjoy seeing how the tree evolves and changes. Just be aware that if you have loads of heavy ornaments or do not like to have your branches settle, you may be better off with an artificial tree.

The final consideration when deciding on a real tree is the length of time you want your tree set up and displayed. Real trees will dry out at some point no matter how well you keep them watered, and they can become fire hazards. I recommend leaving a real tree set up and decorated no longer than four to six weeks for safety purposes. If you need to have your tree up for a longer period of time, you will need to go with an artificial option.

The cost of your tree should be considered when making your decision as well. Real trees do cost considerably less than their artificial counterparts, but it is a recurring yearly investment. On average a real tree is going to cost you anywhere from $25 to $200 every year. An artificial tree costs more up front, but is a longer-term investment.

When it comes to artificial trees, the options in style and function are nearly endless. Artificial trees have come a long way from the wiry, plastic varieties with colored lights from years ago. Newly designed artificial trees are now nearly indiscernible from their real counterparts. If you can think up a color, type, or style, there is someone out there making up your dream tree.

Vintage lovers can select a tinsel tree in any color of their choosing. Rustic types can choose from a large selection of natural-looking pine and fir trees complete with pinecones and berries. If you love the idea of a snow-covered Christmas, check out the beautiful flocked or frosted options. If you are open to something really novel, you can also find upside-down trees that can mount to the wall, sit on a tabletop, or even hang from the ceiling!

When it comes to purchasing your tree, this is another one of those areas where you get what you pay for. The more expensive trees have a higher number of branches, more needles per branch, and often come with warranties on the lights. If you are shopping for a new tree, I encourage you to look at your tree as a long-term investment and purchase the best you can afford at the time. A well-made artificial tree is more realistic and will hold up for many years.

If you are looking to add a second or third tree to your collection, or if you do not have a lot of space, consider purchasing a slim-line tree. These trees give you all of the look and shape of a regular Christmas tree without all of the width. If you are really limited on space, there are beautiful pencil trees, slim-line trees, tabletop trees, and potted varieties that take up very little square footage. No matter your space considerations or style, there is an artificial tree to fit your needs.

Artificial trees do not come with very many cons, but there are a few worth mentioning. Artificial trees need to be stored under conditions that are not overly warm, cold, or damp. These conditions have the potential to rust the frame, short out the lights, and void any warranties. If you usually store your tree in an unventilated attic or cold garage, you need to consider looking for an interior storage space with year-round temperature control.

Artificial trees will also need to be "fluffed" every year when you take them out of storage. Fluffing a tree consists of shaping out the branches and the tips of the tree to look as full as possible. Many of the newly designed trees come preshaped and take minimal fluffing, but if you have an older style, simply take each branch and alternate bending one tip up and the next one down along the length of the branch. This keeps the individual branches as full and realistic looking as possible.

Another con to consider with an artificial tree is the lack of that real tree smell. You can manually replace the smell through a variety of ways. Some companies offer tree-scented fragrance packs that you can nestle in the tree's branches that omit a tree-like aroma. However, I recommend shying away from any artificial fragrances if at all possible.

My favorite solution for replacing that realistic tree smell actually comes from a real tree farm! The Bedrock Tree Farm has spent several years capturing their customers' requests to turn that fresh-from-the-tree farm smell into a candle that can burn throughout the season. After several failed attempts to capture the true essence of the tree in a fragrance, they finally discovered the secret. They combined real tree particles and pure essential oils in a natural soy wax. The result is a truly amazing fragrance that perfectly captures the smell of the Christmas tree.

When it comes down to the final decision on whether or not to decorate with a real or artificial tree, the decision is yours and yours alone. Base your decision on where you are right now and your needs. I personally use a real tree, and I decorate several real trees every year, but many of my clients choose an artificial tree. No matter what you decide, your finished product will be beautiful as you follow the decorating steps to come!

5 | Lighting Your Tree

In the last chapter, we covered all of the ins and outs of selecting your tree. Now that you have made that decision, it is time to move on to getting your tree lit for the world to see! If you decided to go with a real tree, then you will need to take extra notes in this chapter, but even if you purchased an artificial tree, there are still several factors to consider when it comes to your lights.

To start, let's talk about stringing lights onto a real tree. (If you have an artificial tree, please still reference this chapter, since I will be discussing new advancements in lighting technology that will be beneficial to you as well.) Let's take some time to discuss new lighting options on the market today. Christmas tree light technology is changing and improving almost as fast as the home lighting market. The 100-strand, incandescent lights (the industry standard only a few short years ago) are being phased out by LED strands.

LED lights take a lot less energy to run and produce a lot less heat, which is a very good thing when considering their placement near dry pine needles. I was originally not a huge fan of LED lights when they first hit the market. LED lights were too bright, the colored lights were too intense, and the white lights gave off a strange blue glow.

However, in the last few years, retailers have demanded better quality LED Christmas lights, and the manufacturers have listened. Some of my favorite lights on the market today are the Snake or Cluster string lights from RAZ Imports. These lights come in several different lengths on different colored wire (clear or green) as well as colored lights, warm white lights, or even battery options.

The lights themselves are tiny "fairy lights" that blend in beautifully with the tree. They come equipped with a remote control that allows you to set a timer or program

them to eight different settings including steady on, soft fade, and a gentle twinkle (my favorite). My favorite feature about these lights though is their durability. The lights are LED so they last approximately 60,000 hours (that's a lot of Christmas parties!), and they are so well made they can be dropped and even stepped on without damaging the lights. That's my kind of Christmas light!

When deciding on colored or white lights, take the theme or style of your tree into consideration. Colored lights are fun for children's trees, vintage or 1950s nostalgia trees, and for themes with a variety of figurines or characters. The majority of other tree styles and themes look best with classic, warm white lights. White lights complement, instead of compete with, trees that have a variety of elements or that are going for a more "finished" result.

If you decide to go with the standard strands of LED lights, make sure you purchase "warm" white lights in order to ensure a soft white light. Once you decide on your lights, it is time to get them on your tree! For years, I simply did the "wrap one strand around the tree at a time" approach, and I was always frustrated when the branches began to droop halfway through the season, leaving large "black holes."

Designer Tip: Wrapping your lights from the back of the branch, all the way to the tip, and back again, will ensure your tree will remain brightly and evenly lit even when the branches start to droop.

Luckily, a client turned me onto a much better technique for lighting real trees. This client purchases a particularly massive real tree (over 12' tall!) every year and requests that we wrap each and every branch individually. While this approach does take more time, and a lot more lights, the end result is spectacular! There are never any dark holes as the branches sink because each branch is wrapped in light from front to back.

To wrap your individual branches you will need approximately 100–150 individual lights for every foot of tree. While that seems like a lot, the bottom of the tree is quite thick and can really eat up some lights! If you decide to wrap the trunk (more about this to come), you need to add an extra couple of strands to your estimate.

Start your branch wrapping at the bottom of your tree at the back of the lowest branch and simply wrap the lights around the branch all the way to the tip and back again. I like to attach the lights onto the tip of the branch with a dark green pipe cleaner or floral wire to keep the lights from sagging. Once you get back to the trunk, shift over to the next branch and repeat.

One very important thing to remember when lighting any tree is to never plug more than two or three light strands consecutively together. It is also important to never plug more than five to seven strands of connected lights into one power strip or outlet. (You do not want your lights to melt your power strip! Don't ask me how I know this . . .) When you are finished, you will be cursing me for the amount of work this step takes, but praising me for how amazing your tree looks!

The final tip I have for lighting a real tree is to take a picture on your phone of your lights before you begin to decorate. A picture of your tree will often reveal dark holes or areas that need additional lights, whereas the naked eye may be unable to see the bare spots. It is so much easier to add in an additional strand or two of lights at this point, rather than after your tree is fully decorated!

If you decide to use a prelit artificial tree, you are not completely off the tree-lighting hook. Have you ever considered adding some extra lights to jazz things up on your tree? If not, you may want to give it a try. Extra lighting is always appreciated around the holidays when it gets dark so early in the evenings, and it can really add a "wow" element to your tree.

Some fun lighting techniques to try on an artificial tree include wrapping the trunk with colored lights to add a little bit of depth to the darkest part of your tree. I have had clients use red, green, and even multicolored lights wrapped around the trunk with white lights all over the rest of the tree, and the look is very custom and unique.

If you want to add a little magic or romance to your tree, consider adding a couple of strands of the twinkling snake or cluster lights to your prelit tree. These lights are so easy to mix in with existing lights and really add pizzazz to the tree. All you have to do is loosely drape them in and out of the branches to create an extraspecial effect. Another fun trick is to wrap plain wooden branches with these smaller strands of lights and have the branches come out of the tree for a major "wow" factor.

Lighting Ideas for Extra Sparkle:

- Wrap colored lights around the trunk for added depth.
- String twinkle lights in and out of the branches for a magical feel.
- Mix in a few strands of larger round or old-fashioned bulbs for a vintage touch.
- Tuck lighted branches into your topper to add extra "wow" factor to the top of the tree.
- Add in a few strands of solid, colored lights in an accent color to jazz up white lights.
- Hang lighted ornaments on the tree for an unexpected source of light.

If you want to add an extraspecial touch to your tree lights, look into the Magic Light Wand. Just as the name implies, this amazing device is a Christmas Elf's dream come true! Simply plug your lights into the included adapter, wave your magic wand, and voilà! Your Christmas tree magically lights up, and the children know that you are for sure truly magical!

The Magic Light Wand Company describes their wand best:

> *The Magic Light Wand is a whimsical and fun interactive way to turn on your holiday lights. No longer will you flip a switch behind the tree, or press an awkward floor button, or search for a tiny remote—Now you have the Magic Light Wand with light and sound!*

After owning a Magic Light Wand for a few years now, my only tip is to buy more than one. My kiddos fight over who gets to use the wand, so they each have their own color Light Wand now! I also use a Wand for my hard-to-reach mantle decor, and it makes turning my decorations on and off so much more enjoyable!

The final tip I have for adding magic through your lights is to shop for beautiful ornaments that have lighted elements. Battery-lighted options are popping up all over the marketplace, and the battery life lasts longer than ever before with the switch to LED bulbs. A flickering faux candle, minilantern, or color changing ball ornament adds just another layer of fun and sparkle to your tree, and these features often become the most talked-about items on the tree!

Whether or not you have a real or an artificial tree, selecting and applying the right lights can really make or break the finished look. Take a minute here to break out your ***Custom Christmas Tree-Decorating Checklist*** and complete the section on Lighting.

Now that you know about the latest advancements in lighting technology and how to apply them to your tree, it is time to move on to the next layer of your Christmas tree. Keep reading to learn everything you ever wanted to know and more about garlands, decorative mesh, and ribbon wrapping!

"Christmas is a season for kindling the fire for hospitality in the hall, the genial flame of charity in the heart."

-Washington Irving

6 | Adding Movement

In the last chapter, we learned about which kind of lights to choose and how to apply them to your tree. In this chapter, we will dive into the first decorative element that we will add to your tree! This element keeps the eye moving from the top to the bottom of the tree. This element is your garlands, decorative mesh, or wrapped ribbon.

Why do I tell you to make this your very first decorative layer? Through the years of decorating trees, I have discovered that you want your garlands and wrapped ribbon to be nestled into the tree and not wrapped near the end, where it will block your beautiful ornaments and look cluttered.

Designer Tip: Tucking your garland or wrapped ribbon into the tree adds extra depth, movement, and texture. Adding these elements first creates a lovely backdrop for the rest of your ornaments and decorations.

The first step to using garlands, decorative mesh, or wrapped ribbon is selecting which item will work best for your look. Each of these items serve the purpose of adding visual movement to the tree. Garlands are the most popular item in this category, as they come in endless styles and options.

Traditional trees can choose from glass ball garlands, elegant crystal garlands, or colored beaded garlands. Natural trees can select from a variety of mixed greenery garlands, cotton garlands, birch garlands, and moss garlands. If you want a nostalgic look, go for shiny-bright style garlands, country-cloth chain garlands, or even faux popcorn garlands. No matter your style or theme, you can find a garland that will add personality to your tree.

If you want help filling your tree without a large investment, then you might want to consider decorative mesh. This is the same material that has been used to make festive wreaths for years, and it works just as well on your Christmas tree.

In order to select your mesh, all you have to do is select a color that matches your tree's look and "fluff" it up into bunches to tuck into your tree. I like to use pipe cleaners to hold my "fluffs" into place so they are spaced evenly and don't fall flat throughout the season.

Wrapped ribbon is another beautiful option for adding movement to your tree. Wrapped ribbon is exactly what it sounds like, ribbon that is wrapped around your tree in place of a garland. Personally, I am a big fan of ribbon, as three to four bolts of 10-yard ribbon is all you need to wrap a standard 7½' tree. This option gives you a very cost-effective option with a big bang. Ribbon is especially nice on a tree, as it can add three elements at once. Your ribbon can add softness, color, and pattern to your tree all with one item!

More Bang for Your Buck: A coordinating ribbon is a cost-effective tool for decorating your tree. A few bolts of ribbon can be used for a garland on the tree, a bow for your topper, and even decorative accents on your wrapped packages under the tree!

When selecting your ribbon for wrapping your tree, wider ribbon will have more impact. Always attempt to purchase wired ribbon, as you can wrap it into the tree and it will hold its shape. Ribbon can also add needed texture to your tree. If your tree is made up of mostly hard elements, consider adding a textured ribbon such as velvet, burlap, or satin to soften the look and create contrast.

While not every tree will utilize garlands, decorative mesh, or ribbon wrapping, they are wonderful design tools to create a sense of movement on your tree. A well-placed garland or ribbon can move the eye from the top of the tree, back down to the bottom, and up again.

When placing your garlands, ribbon, or decorative mesh, you will usually apply them in a diagonal wrap on your tree, starting at the top of the tree and spiraling downward. Depending on the size of your tree and the thickness of your material, the individual wraps should be about 18" to 3' apart. The larger your tree or the thicker your material, the farther apart your diagonal lines can be wrapped.

If you want a more "casual" or "artsy" look, feel free to tuck your garland, ribbon, or decorative mesh into the tree at random intervals every few feet. You can also tuck your ribbon into the tree and create beautiful movement by "weaving" the ribbon in and out of the branches at regular intervals.

If you are on the fence about whether or not your tree needs a garland, mesh, or ribbon element, consider these questions:

- Do I have a variety of textures on my tree already (hard and soft)?
- Does my tree have enough movement or directional lines?
- Is my color or theme clearly displayed?
- Are there gaps or holes in my finished design?

If you answered yes to any of the above questions, then you may want to consider adding one of these elements to your tree this year! Now, go to your Custom Christmas Tree-Decorating Checklist for an idea of how many of these items to purchase for your tree and jot down the type you will be utilizing.

In this chapter, we have covered three different types of materials that you can use to wrap your tree and learned why we apply them to the tree first. Now it is time to move onto my favorite chapter! In the next chapter, I am going to give you my "Designer Secret" to a perfectly laid-out and balanced Christmas tree design. This one tip creates the framework you need to implement in order to move forward with the rest of your design.

"At Christmas,
all roads lead home."

-Marjorie Holmes

7 | Uncovering the "Designer Secret" to a Great Tree

What if I told you that there was one seldom-discussed "Designer Secret" that could take your tree from blah to fabulous? What if I told you that this tip would help you decorate your tree with ease and make the finished result look cohesive and balanced? Would you be interested? Of course you would! So keep reading to learn this exclusive "Designer Secret" to a great tree: the Diamond Technique!

I am sure that you have heard the saying "Diamonds are a girl's best friend." If you are a *Moulin Rouge!* fan, you probably even have the song running through the back of your head right now. (I know I do!) But, have you ever heard that diamonds are a tree's best friend?

Well, you have now! When it comes to decorating a balanced and cohesive Christmas tree, it is essential to have a good framework or foundation. Designing your tree with the Diamond Technique provides you with the framework needed to guide the rest of your design in a cohesive manner.

So, what is this Diamond Technique of which I speak? It is a carefully placed collection of repeating items that create a connected diamond, or harlequin, pattern around your entire tree.

Placing repeating, key elements in this pattern around your tree creates harmony for the eye and provides diamond-shaped "holes" in your tree that are ready to be filled with your decorative items. These diamond-shaped sections now give you allocated places to hang your remaining elements instead of just standing back and hanging them randomly all over your tree.

Example of a Tree Diamond

Designer Tip: Utilizing the "Diamond Technique" provides your tree with a framework that creates balance, harmony, and a sense of order to the overall design.

Now that you understand what the Diamond Tree Technique is, we need to cover what elements you use to build this framework. There are a variety of different items that you can use to create your diamond design, but they all need to meet a few criteria to be effective.

First, the item needs to be unified, all the way around your tree. This allows the diamond to be cohesive and not distracting. Second, the item needs to be scaled large enough to stand out. If you choose a small ornament or pick (a stem of greenery, flowers, or other decorative elements) for this step, it is not going to be noticeable enough to make an impact on your overall design.

A word of advice: do not worry about overwhelming your tree with the diamond design. If you are new to this technique, it may look strange at first, but I promise that by the time you finish the remaining steps, you will forget the diamond pattern is even there! You will be left with a beautifully decorated tree that is balanced and unified. You will notice in the example photos below that you don't even see the diamond pattern in the fully decorated tree!

(Tree Diamond on tree)   *(Same tree fully decorated)*

Third, select an item that supports your chosen theme or style. Since this is an element that you are going to display in a prominent place and repeat on your tree, make sure that it enforces the desired theme or style that you have chosen. Now that you have an idea of what kind of item you are looking for to create your tree diamond, let's go over some examples to get you started.

One of the easiest items to use to create your diamond is a beautifully tied bow in a ribbon that enforces your theme or style. Bows can be tied to the correct size (a 4–6 loop bow is usually the right size for a standard 7½' tree) and are easy to tie into place exactly where you want them on your tree.

If you are using a bow as your topper (we will talk more about toppers in Chapter 10), then that will be the top bow in your diamond. You will not need to place another bow directly below the topper bow in order to create the design. If you decide to use bows to create your diamond, I recommend that you stay away from wrapping your tree in ribbon as well, as it can be overwhelming.

My favorite item to use when creating the diamond pattern for my clients is a "Tree Bouquet."

Definition: Tree Bouquet
A combination of items such as ribbon, greenery, or flowers that is bundled together to create an arrangement that is used on the tree to make up the "Tree Diamond." The use of multiple bouquets creates a sense of unity in the overall design of the tree.

Tree bouquets can be made out of a wide variety of materials and can be customized to fit any tree style or theme. When creating a tree bouquet, I usually begin with two or three base picks that are what I call "filler" picks. Filler picks are usually picks that are less decorative and more basic in design. Once you have your base picks, you will need one accent piece for each bouquet. Your accent piece will be a more decorative element such as a flower pick or a berry pick.

For example, in a natural or lodge-style tree, your base pick may be a pine pick with a decorative pinecone or berry pick as your accent piece. If you are doing a traditional tree, you may choose a gilded magnolia leaf stem for your base with a colorful poinsettia flower as your accent piece. For a vintage-style tree, glittered branches would be an attractive base for a hydrangea flower accent piece. No matter which style of tree you have, your base pieces should create a foundation that allows your accent piece to "Pop"!

To assemble your tree bouquet, simply place two or three (depending on the size of the pick) base stems flat with the stems crossing each other. Then lay your accent piece (flower, bow, or ornament) on top and either zip-tie or wire your stems together. You will then apply your horizontal bouquets by tucking them into the tree following the diamond pattern.

If you choose to do a coordinating floral topper (discussed more in Chapter 10), you will use that bouquet as your top in the uppermost diamond. When placing tree bouquets into the tree, I only wire them in place if I am decorating a real tree. With artificial trees, I simply tuck the bouquets into the branches, and I have never had an issue with them slipping.

Now that you know the secret to a designer-looking tree, it's time to get out your **Custom Christmas Tree-Decorating Checklist** and check out how many bouquets you will need. The number of bouquets needed depends on the size of your tree and whether or not you decide to decorate

your tree all the way around. If you are just decorating the front three-quarters of the tree (if you are putting the back of the tree against the wall or in a corner), you will need fewer bouquets, so keep that in mind during your planning and purchasing stages.

For a standard 7.5' tree you will need, on average, 7–9 tree bouquets for the front ¾ of the tree (but none on the back) and 12–14 bouquets for a fully decorated tree (all the way around). You will need an additional 4–6 bouquets for a 9' tree to complete the design.

Tree bouquets are a really fun element to implement on your tree and can really make a lack-luster-looking tree evolve into a "wow" tree. I do not use tree bouquets on every tree I design, so it is not required, but it is a fun and simple way to make your tree really stand out and look professionally decorated! Now that you have learned the secret to a designer-looking tree, it is time to move on to Chapter 8: Adding Focal Points. What is a focal point and why should you use one? Read on to find out!

"Christmas isn't just a day,
it's a frame of mind."

Valentine Davies,
Miracle on 34th Street

8 | Adding Focal Points

Now that you have completed the previous steps, you have a tree that is beautifully lit, wrapped, and structured with your diamond design. Now is the time to start adding your decorative pieces into the tree itself. Before you grab your box of ornaments, there is one more special element to consider: the focal point.

Focal points are items on your tree that are larger-scaled than normal, often unexpected, and only used in moderation. These pieces add that special "wow" factor to your tree and draw people in to check out more. Focal points can be anything that carries out your theme or style and that can be wired, tied, or attached to your tree.

Designer Tip: Children love unexpected focal points on Christmas trees! If you plan on entertaining youngsters this holiday season, think up some fun items that you can tuck into your tree to guarantee some extra squeals and giggles from your youngest guests.

I personally love to use focal points on my clients' trees, because they add so much personality to the finished design. Focal pieces also help to balance out the scale of all of the small ornaments, as they are larger and more prominently placed on the tree. These items are often things that you would not normally consider putting on a tree. When you are trying to brainstorm what to use as your focal point, put on your creativity cap! Think about your theme and what kind of item you could place on your tree to create a fun and unexpected focal point.

Here are some examples that may get your creative wheels turning:

* ❄ A large-scale woodland animal such as a reindeer, moose, fox, or owl for a woodland-themed tree.

* ❄ A pair of cross-country skis or a vintage sled for a lodge-themed tree.

* ❄ Large angels wired into a traditional or inspirational tree.

* ❄ Oversize, wrapped candy pieces tucked into a kitchen- or Candyland-themed tree.

* ❄ Lanterns with battery candles hanging on a Southern-themed tree.

* ❄ Baskets or wrapped paper cones filled with ruffled flowers on a vintage or romantic tree.

* ❄ Large, glittered branches coming out of a Winter Wonderland-themed tree.

* ❄ Elves or large Santa Clauses wired into a Santa-themed tree.

* ❄ Toy trains, teddy bears, and jack-in-the-boxes wired into a children's tree.

* ❄ Packages wrapped in festive paper tucked into the branches of a mix-and-matched family tree.

* ❄ Decorative harps, trumpets, and horns adorning a carolers- or music-themed tree.

As you can see, the options for focal points are endless, and one with a unique element can add so much fun to your tree!

When it comes to placing your focal points, I usually limit myself to one really special item or, at the most, three to five pieces placed in alternating "holes" in my diamond pattern, which is explained in the last chapter. If I'm not using a diamond pattern, I place my focal pieces in a loose zigzag pattern on the front of the tree to keep the eye moving up and down the branches. I do not recommend placing focal pieces toward the back or too far into the tree as they are meant to be pieces that really pop.

Don't fret if you can't think of a focal point for your tree! Not every tree needs to feature focal points, so simply don't add them in if they do not fit with your overall design.

Now that you are brainstorming some fun pieces that you can tuck into your tree, it is time to get out your **_Custom Christmas Tree-Decorating Checklist_** and fill out what your focal point element is going to be and how many you are going to incorporate!

"It is Christmas
in the heart that puts
Christmas in the air."

-W. T. Ellis

9 | Hanging the Ornaments

Can you believe that we are in chapter 9 of the book and just now hanging our first ornament?!? If your normal routine consists of stringing some lights, hanging some ornaments, and calling it a tree, then I am sure that this has been an adjustment for you. I promise you can get to hanging all of the ornaments your heart desires very soon! But first, we need to spend a little time breaking down the different types of ornaments that you will need to really maximize your tree's potential.

While selecting your ornaments might seem simple enough, there is actually more to it than you would think. It is important to have a wide selection of different styles of ornaments to keep your tree balanced and full. When it comes to selecting ornaments, you need to make sure to have a variety of three key components: size, texture, and shape. This is very important because if your ornaments are all limited to a similar size, material, and/or shape, it is challenging to get the depth and dimension that your tree needs to really come together into a complete and pleasing design.

> By purchasing ornaments in a variety of sizes, shapes, and textures, you are creating a collection that will make your tree look full and visually pleasing.

We are going to start off talking about the importance of using a variety of different-sized ornaments and how to place them on the tree. When you get your

ornaments out and look them over, I bet you will find that the vast majority of your ornaments are in the 2"–4" range. While there is nothing wrong with smaller ornaments, it is important to mix in some larger ornaments for scale. I recommend having several ornaments in a variety of larger sizes (6"–10") to help balance out the lower portion of your tree. The base of the tree is wider and deeper and therefore requires larger ornaments to fill appropriately.

Designer Tip: Placing large, reflective ornaments deep in the branches will help save you money in the long run. The larger ornaments fill the bigger holes for less money than lots of smaller ornaments, and the reflective surface acts as a mirror reflecting back everything that hangs in front!

Another one of my favorite Designer Secrets is to purchase some really large 200 mm (8" or close to soccer-ball size!) plastic or shatterproof ornaments to tuck way back into the bottom branches. This makes such a huge difference on the tree because it fills in those deep bottom branches and acts like a mirror reflecting the lights back out of the darkest part of your tree. While it may seem silly to purchase ornaments that large for a regularly sized tree, do not be afraid! You will be surprised at what a difference it makes and thankful you gave it a try!

Once you have evaluated your existing ornaments for size, it is important to look them over for a variety of materials/textures as well. Most trees are decorated with predominantly glass ornaments. If you are looking for a balanced and full tree, you need to intentionally add in ornaments with a variety of different textures. Carved wooden ornaments, woolly animals, feathered birds, crystal icicles, and metal carvings are just a few ideas of the different textures that you can incorporate on your tree.

In addition to a variety of sizes and textures, a well-decorated tree will have a variety of shapes as opposed to one or two shapes repeated over and over. If you are like most of my clients, you probably have an abundance of round balls and maybe a few other shapes thrown in for good measure.

If you fall into this group, make a point to pick up some additional shapes when you go shopping for new ornaments.

Some other shapes to look for include:

- Teardrops
- Onions
- Flat cutouts
- Disks
- Snowflakes
- Figurines
- Stars
- Icicles

There are a lot of companies that sell sets of coordinating ornaments in different shapes if you need a premixed option.

Now that you have taken the time to evaluate your ornaments for a variety of sizes and shapes, it is time to get them on the tree!

When hanging your ornaments, make sure you hang them from back to front as well as top to bottom. If you hang all of your ornaments on the outer branches, your tree will look one-dimensional and will lack depth. Hang the ornaments that are showing signs of age or wear near the back and save your favorite or theme ornaments for front and center!

In order to get a good mix of ornaments throughout your tree, it is helpful to lay them out and organize them into groups based on size or type. Then you can spread each group out over the tree to keep from getting too many of a similar ornament in one area. My favorite way to do this is to set up a folding table in the room with the tree and lay the ornaments into groups on an old blanket or towel. This brings them up to an easy-to-reach height, and when you are finished, you simply wash your blanket or towel: less mess and less back strain!

Luckily, the diamond technique we discussed earlier has set the framework for hanging your ornaments. Simply hang one ornament of each shape and size in each diamond-shaped section and repeat. This process allows your ornaments to be placed in an organized and balanced manner. Continue until you are out of ornaments or your tree reaches your desired fullness. (I am not sure that I have ever had ornaments left over, but I do like a full tree!)

If you have a collection of favorite ornaments from years past, do not feel like you have to banish them to the attic if you want to try a new tree style or theme! I always ask my clients to have their own ornaments out whenever I come to decorate their tree. I love to include the history and memories these special ornaments represent. If you want to try a new look, it is very easy to update your existing ornaments by investing in multiples of two to three new theme ornaments and updating your garlands or other themed elements.

For example, if you have a collection of mismatched ornaments that you have collected through the years, but you decide that you want to decorate in a Rustic style this year, simply go through your ornaments and pull out any that would coordinate with your new style as well as any family favorites that hold special meaning.

Shopping Tip: All you need to update your existing tree to a new theme or style is 5–10 coordinated ornaments, some new ribbon, and a few accent picks. A few key pieces can result in a big update!

Then decide on two or three ornaments in your new style to add to your tree and purchase 5–10 of each ornament. For example, for a Rustic tree, you could purchase eight birch snowflakes, six tin stars, and seven metal bells to coordinate into your tree and blend all of your miscellaneous ornaments into the new look. Then simply update one or two other elements and you have an entirely new look using a lot of your existing ornaments!

When updating your theme, remember the importance of purchasing enough ornaments in your new theme or style to allow the eye to connect the elements and create a sense of unity. Purchasing three ornaments in a variety of styles will not be enough to make a real impact, and you will feel disappointed with the end result. If you are dividing out your tree budget over a few years, I recommend investing in several of one ornament every year instead of purchasing ornaments at random. Once you have firmly established your theme or style, you can begin to add in one ornament at a time.

If you have a lot of leftover ornaments that you did not utilize on your new tree, think about where you could place a minitree in your home. Small trees add such personality to a kitchen, guest room, or master bedroom and are great places to utilize your extra ornaments. Extra ornaments can also be used to decorate wreaths and mantle garlands or tucked into centerpieces and tabletop displays, so there is no need to let your extra ornaments go to waste!

The final thing we are going to cover when it comes to ornaments is the actual hanging device. Unless you have a nonbreakable or fabric ornament, do not hang it with the gold thread that comes with most ornaments! It is not a reliable hanging mechanism, and I have seen too many beautiful ornaments broken because the thread broke or the knot came loose!

I often invest in the decorative packs of ornament hooks with the small hook on one end and the swirled end on the other. Attach these hooks to the actual top of the ornament and they will give you more insurance against falls. If you have a real tree, I recommend wiring breakable or heavy ornaments to the branches with floral wire or brown pipe cleaners to protect them as the branches start to droop.

Now that we have finally covered all of the ins and outs of ornaments for your tree, take some time to look over which ornaments you currently have and what you need to add to complete your look. Log this information into your ***Custom Christmas Tree-Decorating Checklist*** so you have a record, and remember to shop early for best selection! In the next chapter, we are going to cover one of the most overlooked parts of the tree—the topper!

10 | Designing a Custom Topper

Congratulations! By now, your tree is really starting to come together, and I hope you are in love with the results. We are now going to dive into the one area of the tree where the vast majority of my clients and customers have made major improvements on their trees.

The section that almost always needs improvement is the tree topper. When I teach classes on Tree Decorating, I always offer one important tip about the tree: if you do nothing else to your tree this year, update your topper. I guarantee you, focusing on this one area will update and refresh the most tired of trees. It really is that important of an element, as the top sets the mood for the entire rest of the tree!

In order to be sure we are on the same page, let me clarify what I mean by a tree topper. A topper for a tree is the single item or combination of pieces that are used to "finish off" the top of the tree. This is often a bow, star, or some other type of element attached to the uppermost part of the tree.

While I seldom see a tree without any top decoration at all, I almost always see trees with toppers that are less than exciting. In the paragraphs below I will teach you all of my tips and techniques to get a topper that really grabs attention and sets your tree apart from the crowd.

Definition: Tree Topper
A single item or combination of items that is placed on the top of the tree to add decoration.

To begin, I am going to try to get you to open your mind about what a tree topper is supposed to look like. While a single bow, star, angel, or finial is fine, there is so much opportunity to do something really special with your topper. Your tree topper sets the stage for the look and style of the rest of your tree, so it is important to give it the attention it deserves.

As a Tennessee gal, I like to compare my tree topper to a Southern woman's hair: the bigger the hair, the closer to Jesus! While I say this somewhat jokingly, it is often true. A big, full topper helps balance your tree, enforces your theme or style, and really "tops off" your entire tree.

In order to create a great, full topper, you usually need a combination of three factors: height, fullness, and a center point. The height element makes up the center of the topper and brings the eye all the way up your tree and beyond. Pieces that add height to a topper are branches and taller picks.

The fullness element adds visual weight and balance to the topper. For pieces that add fullness, I usually turn to shorter picks that help coordinate my theme or style. Flower stems are good choices to add fullness to the top if they fit your look and overall design. If you are utilizing the Diamond Technique from Chapter 7, be sure to include some of the same picks in your topper to coordinate your entire look!

Finally, the center point brings all of the elements together and serves as a transition from the tree itself into the topper. The center point of your topper is usually your bow, angel, star, or other main decorative element. I love to use my client's existing topper as the center element in many cases. This balance of old and new allows you to use what you love, while giving it a whole new look!

If you do not already have a center point to start from, brainstorm your theme and think about some fun options. In my own home, we used a Santa's hat as our tree topper before we found the lighted star that we currently use, and I have seen adorable snowmen-themed trees with top hats as a topper. Small decorative wreaths can be attached to the top for a unique look, and large scale ornaments can be tied into the center of bows to form an easy and custom topper.

Now that you know about some of the many materials that can be used to assemble your topper, it is time to design a topper that is unique to you. When it comes to deciding on a custom topper for your tree there are a few things to consider. Take some time to evaluate your tree and ask yourself these questions:

❋   How much space do I have from the top of the tree to the ceiling?

❋   Which elements would pull my theme or style together?

❋   Is my tree balanced or is it bottom-heavy? (Since trees are cone-shaped, they are almost always skinny at the tops and wide at the bottoms.)

❋   Is the top of my tree too dark?

Once you have answered all of these questions, it is time to brainstorm a topper design that is perfect for your tree. Let's break the questions down one by one and discuss the factors you will want to consider when planning your custom tree topper.

QUESTION #1: HOW MUCH SPACE DO I HAVE FROM THE TOP OF MY TREE TO THE CEILING?

The answer to this question will guide you in how tall to make your topper. If you have a standard 7½' tree and 8' ceiling, you will usually have around 1' of space for your topper. (Your tree is measured to the very tip, so you usually have an extra 6"–8" of usable decorating space in addition to the finished measurement.)

If you have a smaller tree or taller ceilings, then you will have plenty of space for your topper. If you have limited height, simply tuck your picks into the tree farther down from the very top. This way you can still have a great-looking topper in a tight space. A standard rule of thumb is the taller the ceilings, the taller you can make your topper.

QUESTION #2: WHICH ELEMENTS CAN I USE TO PULL MY THEME OR STYLE TOGETHER?

If you have a particular theme or style that you are trying to enforce, your topper is the perfect place to really go all out. Depending on the style or theme of your tree, there are loads of different choices.

For a rustic, lodge, or cabin-styled tree consider adding bare branches for height, a natural berry or greenery pick for fullness, and a grapevine star or plaid-checked bow for the center. Romantic or vintage trees can be inspired by glittered feathers for height, ruffled flowers for fullness, and a soft, fabric angel or big, lush bow for the center. Traditional trees can choose from an endless variety of picks for the height and fullness and a star, bow, finial, or angel for the center.

If you have a themed tree you can really have some fun selecting your materials! Christmas stores are constantly getting in new and unexpected items that you can utilize to create fun and memorable toppers. For a snowman tree, look for a top hat and picks with little snowballs or snow-flakes attached. A Santa-themed tree stands out with a Santa hat topper and a big buckle print bow. Candyland trees can be perfected with a combination of candy cane picks and striped candy streamers.

One of my favorite toppers that sticks out in my memory comes from a bird-themed tree. For this client we hot-glued nests and reindeer moss onto bare tree branches and clipped on a variety of realistic-looking faux birds. When we wired those branches into the top of the tree, it was truly transformed from fun to absolutely fabulous!

QUESTION #3: IS MY TREE BALANCED OR IS IT BOTTOM-HEAVY?

Christmas trees are, by their very nature, skinny at the tops and wide at the bottoms. This can make your tree appear very bottom-heavy if you do not intentionally balance out the top.

Designing a topper that fans out or branches out at the top can help to provide balance for the wider bottom and make a more pleasing whole. To create the fan shape, simply angle your middle-layer filler picks so that they come out of the sides of the top in a fan-like shape. This adds much-needed fullness to the top of the tree.

QUESTION #4: IS THE TOP OF MY TREE DARK?

This question ties into the previous question we discussed. Since trees are narrower at the top, there are naturally fewer lights. If you add picks and a bow to your topper, you can often be left with a dark spot on the top of your tree. Thankfully, there are some really wonderful products out there to combat this problem.

Electric lighted branches can be tucked into your topper arrangement and will really bring your topper to life. These branches come in several different styles including natural, moss-covered, flocked, glittered, and more. Adding lighted branches to your topper is easy. Simply tuck them into

the center of your topper arrangement and mold the branches into your desired shape. Then run your plug down the tree and plug it into the same power strip or cord as your lights.

Another way to add light to the top of your tree is by incorporating a lighted topper into your arrangement. Lighted angels and stars are the most common and direct our focus toward the real reason for the season. If an angel or star does not fit your decor, there are many different options to consider. Lighted toppers allow you to add a larger, more focused light onto the top of your tree and prevent a black hole effect.

My favorite lighted topper comes from Starry Treasures, a company that makes beautiful lighted Moravian Star toppers out of glass. These stars are beautiful on their own, but when you turn the lights on, the result is truly mesmerizing. Starry Treasures makes all of their own products (toppers, ornaments, and overhead lighting) and sources all of their glass in the United States. Their glass stars come on a sturdy metal pole and can easily be attached to the trunk of the tree with zip ties.

If your tree theme or style calls for a simpler topper, that is fine as well! Just be sure that your topper carries your theme up to the top of the tree, and that the scale of the topper is pleasing to the overall design. Sometimes, simply increasing the size and scale of an existing topper is enough to update a tree and give it a new look.

Now that you have answered all of the Tree Topper questions, it is time to attach your topper to the tree. If you are using a traditional star, angel, or finial, I recommend attaching it to the tree first, then filling in behind and around the topper with your picks, attaching your bow last (if using one).

For a topper that is a combination of picks, flowers, and/or bows, I find it easier to arrange the pieces first and wire or pipe-cleaner them together. Then attach the entire arrangement to the tree with a zip tie to keep it from falling. If you are incorporating a bow into your topper, I usually place one bow on the front and one on the back of the tree to create balance and to cover the stems or supports of the topper.

If you are wondering why I save this step toward the end, the answer comes in keeping your topper straight. Once your topper is straight and attached to your tree, you do not want to bump or jostle your tree. Getting up and down the ladder ten times to straighten your topper will very quickly take the fun out of decorating!

For that reason, I always recommend having someone available on the ground to help you line up your topper when it is time to attach. It is nearly impossible to gauge straightness when you are on a ladder leaning over a tree! If your tree is front-heavy (if you don't decorate the back) or if you are using a real tree, now is the time to anchor your tree as well. I highly recommend tying your tree off to a wall or window casing if there is any concern at all that your tree could fall. I had my tree fall one year, and trust me: you do not want that to happen!

Designer Tip: Anchoring your tree to a wall, windowsill, or other sturdy surface is an important step you don't want to skip. Christmas trees can easily become front-heavy, as there are often more decorations up front and you don't want that weight to pull your tree over!

In order to tie off your tree, I recommend using monofilament fishing line since it is clear. Purchase a heavier weight to ensure enough strength to hold your tree. Then, simply wrap the line around the top of the tree and attach it to a small O-ring anchored into the wall or window trim. This one step may save you hours of clean-up and hundreds of dollars of broken ornaments down the road!

By now you should have a pretty clear picture in your mind of the look and style you want for your tree topper. Take time now to fill out the Tree Topper section in your *Custom Christmas Tree-Decorating Checklist.* Be sure to purchase your items ahead of time so you have them available when it is time to decorate!

Once your topper is attached and looking great, it is time to move onto the final step of your tree-decorating journey. In the next chapter, we are going to have fun creating a firm foundation with the base of our tree. See you there!

"When they saw the star,
they rejoiced!"

Matthew 2:10

11 | Coordinating Your Base

In the last chapter, we discussed the importance of maximizing the topper on your tree to really bring your look together. In this chapter, we are going to discuss another often-overlooked portion of the tree, the base. The base of your tree is the foundation of your entire look and, as such, needs to be considered in your overall design.

When decorating a room, I remind clients to consider the whole picture. You are designing your room from the ground to the ceiling. The same is true in tree design. You leave so much decorating potential out there if you neglect the base of your tree!

Decorating the base of your tree allows you to carry your theme or style all the way down to the bottom of your design. If you are using a real tree, you need to consider the possibility of getting water on your pieces. Luckily, there are many new devices available now to aid in watering your tree, so this is no longer an issue. If you have an artificial tree, there are fewer limitations on what you can utilize for your base.

One of my favorite things to do with my base is use it to elevate my tree. If you have additional space at the top of your tree, consider lifting your tree up on an elevated base to really give your tree presence. You can do this by placing your tree on a sturdy platform such as a wooden box. You can also place your tree into a sturdy urn, barrel, or planter to elevate the tree. Decorative tree bases designed to hold artificial trees are hard to find, but if you can find one, they elevate the tree and add a lot of fun to the base.

Lifting your tree up and adding a tall topper is a very economical way to take a small tree and transform it into a much more impressive, finished piece. I often tell my clients not to purchase a 9' tree for a room with 9' ceilings, but rather, to purchase a 7 ½' tree so they have room to elevate the tree and add a great topper. Elevating your tree also opens up more floor space for train sets, themed displays, and gifts, which is always a good thing!

Designer Tip: To create a really special effect on the base of your elevated tree, hang layers of different styles and icicles all over the bottom branches. This creates a beautiful and reflective layered look that is elegant, dramatic, and unexpected!

I remember one memorable house that I decorated with soaring ceilings. My client purchased a fully decorated tree from our store and hired me to deliver and decorate the tree in her formal living room. After setting the tree up and decorating it to the nines, it still looked dwarfed in her massive room. What to do? We did a quick look around her house and grabbed a small dining table from her sitting room. We then proceeded (with lots of help) to lift the entirely decorated tree up on top of her round dining table! The finished result was spectacular, and she told me this is where her tree goes every year now.

If your ceilings do not allow for towering trees, but you still want something special, consider a rotating tree stand. Rotating stands allow you to put the entire tree on display and are perfect for those with a large ornament collection. When using a rotating stand, remember, the entire tree needs to be evenly decorated, so your tree diamond and your topper will need to continue all the way around. The right location is also essential for a rotating tree. Trees on rotating stands need to be placed in a corner or near a wall where they can be plugged in, but far enough out that the tree does not touch anything. A quick word of caution: rotating stands are usually limited to 7 ½' artificial trees, and you do not want to test those limits!

If you are using a real tree and want to add some "wow" factor to your base, don't feel left out. You can add a lot of impact to your look by selecting a coordinated tree skirt or other fabric element; tree skirts are available in so many fun designs. Etsy is a great place to look for unique designs that coordinate with your tree style or theme. Tree skirts can even be customized with your family's names for a personalized touch.

If you do not wish to invest in a custom tree skirt, consider using festive tablecloths or cut fabric for an inexpensive skirt. Round tablecloths can be purchased in loads of patterns and colors, and can usually be picked up inexpensively from discount stores. Just fold them in half, lay them around the base of the tree, and they are hard to discern from a real tree skirt.

Cost-cutting Tip: Adding a tree skirt to your tree doesn't have to be expensive! Flat sheets, large cuts of fabric, tablecloths, or even an old quilt can be used to create a beautiful base for your tree.

The base of your tree is also a fun place to display favorite collections or pieces that tie into your theme or style. For example, if you have a traditional or family tree, a train chugging along the bottom is almost a must. Staged vignettes with small furniture, planters, baskets, and/or collectibles look great under traditional trees as well.

Rustic or natural style trees can really stand out if you use old crates or wooden boxes to hold the tree. Vintage tin buckets filled with natural greenery branches, wooden crates full of packages, or an old-fashioned sled can anchor and add character to the bottom of the tree.

Romantic-style trees are magical with Christmas villages laid out below the branches with blankets of faux snow nestled all around. Collections of plush figures can add whimsy and delight to a snowman or teddy bear tree. Rustic- or lodge-themed trees can be coordinated with natural baskets full of pinecombs or birch logs stacked around the base to really add that outdoorsy feel!

If you have an elegant or color-themed tree, consider wrapping boxes in beautiful, coordinated wrapping paper to nestle under the bottom branches. I have clients who store their wrapped "packages" away every year with the rest of their tree decor!

If you are looking for something really unique for under your tree, consider stringing LED lights (important because they stay cool!) into mesh garland and tuck it under your tree in layers. The light twinkling through the mesh is really unexpected and magical!

As a momma to three young boys, I would be remiss if I did not mention another very practical purpose for the base of your tree. If you have young children, dogs with very active tails, or other rambunctious creatures in your home (except for cats: nothing that I've found will keep a determined kitty away), the base of the tree is also the perfect place to create a boundary of sorts if necessary. For several years I have placed a large, folding baby gate around the base of our tree to protect the boys from the glass ornaments and the glass ornaments from the boys! It may not be the "prettiest" look around, but it certainly serves its purpose.

No matter how you decide to dress the base of your tree, the important thing is to give it a little extra attention so that it accentuates the rest of your overall design. Take a minute right now to fill out the "Tree Base" section on your ***Custom Christmas Tree-Decorating Checklist***, and now we are on our way to the last chapter in the book . . . Finishing Touches!

"He who has not
Christmas in his heart
will never find it
under a tree."

-Roy L. Smith

12 | Finishing Touches

Y ou have arrived at the final chapter on decorating a unique and beautiful Christmas tree. Did you have any idea there was so much that could go into the decorating of a tree? I know I wasn't aware of the number of choices when I started decorating professionally over ten years ago.

In this final chapter, I am going to leave you with some small touches that can have really big results on your Christmas tree. Like all of the other steps, adding these pieces are optional, but I encourage you to utilize at least one element to really finish off your tree.

When it comes to the finishing touches, I am talking about the pieces that you put on as the very last step. These items go on your tree when you think there is not room for one more item. What kinds of things am I talking about? Well, let's find out!

BRANCH CLIPS: Branch clips are small decorations that are attached to a clip instead of to an ornament hanger. This allows you to place these items way out on the very tip of the branches. I adore branch clips for the way they look suspended on the very edge of the tree, where nothing else can go.

When looking for branch clips, remember to check the weight of the clip. Most are very lightweight, but if they are heavier, they will need to go on sturdier branches or farther into the tree. Branch clips come in a variety of styles including nests, birds, characters such as Santa Clause or snowmen, individual flower blossoms, and even mushrooms! Branch clips can be a little hard to find, so when you see some you like, snatch them up!

LIGHTED CANDLES: When you think back to old-fashioned Christmas trees, you may remember lighted candles on the tree adding warmth and light. While we do not use real candles on trees anymore (at least I hope not!), new technology allows us to add battery-powered candles onto our tree to capture the magic of days gone by. These new candles usually come with clip-on bases so they can be placed wherever you want them on your tree. With a simple click of the remote you can have soft, flickering candles on your tree!

DECORATIVE MINIPICKS: If you have already used garlands and/or tree bouquets, you may not need any additional pieces. However, if you survey your tree and notice any bare spots or holes, you probably do not need more ornaments, but rather, mini-filler picks (small branches of berries, greenery, flowers, or other decorative elements). These pieces are usually in the 4"–5" range and are designed to tuck directly into the tree.

Your minipicks need to coordinate with your style or theme, but do not have to match any of the other picks used. Small berry picks, cotton picks, single flower stems, or glittered leaves make great picks to fill any remaining holes on your tree.

VERTICAL GARLANDS OR RIBBON TENDRILS: If you are looking for something to pull your entire tree together, then consider adding a vertical element. Vertical elements include delicate garlands than can be hung from the top of the tree down as well as ribbon tendrils that start at the top and hang down. Vertical garlands are usually made of beads, crystals, berries, or items such as bells, tied to a string.

Ribbon tendrils can be twisted for a twirled effect or run straight down the tree. This layer of ribbon and garland is added at the very end of the process because you want the pieces to finish off your tree and lie over top of the other decorations. When you hang your vertical elements, I recommend attaching them directly under your topper element. It usually takes a minimum of five vertical garlands to look balanced on your tree, but you can add up to nine depending on the item's size.

ICICLES: Icicles usually fall into two categories. People either love them or cannot stand them. I personally fall into the love category and find their sparkle on the tree irresistible. If you decide to add icicles to your tree, I recommend adding them at the very end to allow them to "drip" off of the tips of your branches. I often wire my icicles onto the very ends of the branch to create that dripping effect.

Icicles come in a wide variety of sizes and materials. For heavily decorated trees, I recommend delicate, spun-glass icicles. Adding a few sets of these to your tree adds a sparkle that I have a hard time replicating with any other item. If you have a Winter Wonderland or other theme where the icicles really add to the overall look, you may want to look into larger plastic or foam icicles that really stand out. If your tree is elevated off the ground, filling the underside of the tree with icicles in different shapes and styles creates a truly magical effect.

OLD-FASHIONED TINSEL: Tinsel is another one of those items that has a love or hate following. I personally love the look of tinsel on a vintage- or 1950s-style tree, even though I have never found a way to use it without the mess!

There really is not anything like the look of a tree decked out in shiny tinsel and collections of family ornaments from years past.

ORNAMENT SPINNERS: If you have never seen an ornament spinner, let me introduce you to this little wonder. Ornament spinners are small devices that plug into the lights on the tree and slowly spin an ornament around in circles. They are a fun way to highlight a special ornament and add additional magic to your tree.

Using ornament spinners is simple enough, but there are some things you need to know. So far the spinners on the market only work with traditional Christmas lights (not LEDs). They work by removing a bulb from the light strand and plugging the spinner into the base. This allows the spinner to run off of the power of the lights.

Ornament spinners are easiest to use on artificial trees, as it is much easier to bend their branches into submission; however, it is possible to use them on a real tree. For use on a real tree, you will need to look for a hole in the branches to place the spinner so the ornament will not bump up against any other branches or decorations.

It is now time to pull out your ***Custom Christmas Tree-Decorating Checklist*** for the last time and fill out the final section on Finishing Touches. Jot down what you want to add to complete your Christmas tree. There is no hard rule on how many of these items to use, but do consider the overall effect on your tree when making your decision.

When deciding what to add to finish your perfect tree, remember that while I do decorate a few trees every year that utilize at least one or two elements from each chapter, you do not have to use

every item listed to create a beautiful tree! Each tree has its own personality, and your style should guide your decisions on what elements to utilize to create a tree that is uniquely yours.

We have now covered the final chapter on the materials and techniques needed to decorate your tree. Congratulations! You are now trained and equipped to decorate your best-looking tree ever! Be sure to invite friends, family, and neighbors over to make memories and enjoy the season around your beautifully decorated tree!

"The best of all gifts
around the Christmas tree:
the presence of a happy family all wrapped up in each
other."

-Burton Hills

13 | Tree Inspiration and Ideas

If you are considering adding a new tree, or fully updating your existing tree this year and need some inspiration on a new look or theme, then this chapter will serve as your inspirational guide. Tackling an entire new tree or redoing an existing tree can seem overwhelming at first, but once you get an idea of your theme, which key elements you need to carry out each theme, and how many of each item you need, then simply follow the steps laid out in this book and you will be well on your way to a fabulously decorated tree!

When working with clients on a new tree design, one question I get consistently asked is:

> "How many lights, bows, garlands, ornaments, tree bouquets, etc., do I need on my tree?"

While there isn't a "set-in-stone" answer to this question, I will provide you with a helpful guide that you can use as a starting point for a full-looking tree. The shopping guide below is for a standard 7½' Christmas tree. The quantities can be adjusted for larger or smaller trees; smaller trees need, on average, ½ to ¾ times as much product as the standard, while 9' trees traditionally need 1½ to 1¾ times as much.

Shopping List for a Standard 7½' Tree:

- **Lights:** approximately 1,000 lights. Can add decorative lights as desired
- **Garlands/Wrapped Ribbon:** 8–10 6' garlands or 20' of ribbon

- **Focal Pieces:** 1–3 for the front/sides only; 5 for a fully decorated tree
- **Tree Bouquets, Bows, or Florals:** 9 for the front/sides only; 15 for fully decorated
- **Large-Diameter Filler Ornaments:** 4–8
- **Medium Filler Ornaments:** 20–30
- **Decorative Theme or Accent Ornaments:** as many as your heart desires
- **Topper:** 1 decorative star, angel, Santa, bow, or finial; 5–7 tall stems; and/or 3–5 shorter picks for a topper bouquet (Stems can be added behind the star, angel, bow, Santa, or finial for a fuller look.)
- **Final Touches:** icicles, branch clips, clip-on candles, etc., added, as desired
- **Base:** tree stand, tub, basket, skirt, or tulle, as desired

If you are considering adding a new tree, or really updating your existing tree, this year and need some inspiration on a new look or theme, then the following list of 35 tree themes will get you started in the right direction! To get you inspired I have included a brief description of the overall style of the tree, along with a list of the top five elements you can use to really get a great start on a new look.

35 HOT DESIGNER TREE THEMES

1. Winter Wonderland

A fresh and woodsy tree that is perfect for leaving up after the holidays all the way through the winter months. Woodland creatures, lots of natural textures, and sparkly "iced" accents keep this look light, organic, and sparkly. This theme looks great on a natural or flocked tree base.

Top 5 Elements:

- Woodland creature figurines/ornaments like owls, foxes, and bears
- Sparkly icicles to hang off branch tips
- Twinkle lights to weave in and out of the tree for a magical effect
- Ornaments featuring bark, feathers, sticks, and other natural elements
- Branches or birch sticks to tuck into the tree and topper

2. Candy Land Christmas

Sweet, fun, and colorful perfectly sum up the feeling of this playful themed tree. Imagine pastel-hued bonbons, peppermint swirled ribbon, and loads of candy-themed ornaments dancing off of a white tinsel tree . . . perfect for a kitchen, kid's room, or playroom!

Top 5 Elements:

- Confectionary and candy-themed ornaments
- Colorful ball or cupcake garlands
- Peppermint strips or pastel polka-dot ribbon
- Decorative picks featuring candies, marshmallows, or pom-poms
- Accent lights in pink, lime green, or multicolored

3. Dickens Carolers

If Christmas brings to mind fur-wrapped carolers sipping mugs of hot cider, then this theme is right up your alley! Rich colors, warm textures, and musical accents create a classic Christmas theme. Perfect for a standard real or artificial green tree.

Top 5 Elements:

- Red, gold, and burgundy glass ornaments
- Rich velvet or fur-accented ribbon
- Caroler figures for focal points
- Musical instrument/note ornaments
- Traditional lamppost branch clips or ornaments

4. Cowboy Christmas

This tree if perfect for a gun-toting cowboy, whether he's one in real-life or just likes watching them in the movies. Earthy Santa Fe-inspired colors and genuine leather accents keep this look authentic, without going "cutesy." This theme is perfect for a slim-line tree, a rugged pine, or a cactus-shaped tree. (Yes, they do exist!)

Top 5 Elements:

- Basic ornaments in rust, mustard, and turquoise
- Leather stars, boots, and/or miniature cowboy hats
- Wire or tin accented lanterns, bells, or stars to tuck into the branches
- Cattle rope, burlap ribbon, or faux barbed wire to wrap as a garland
- Horse shoes, spurs, and miniature wagon wheels to add dimension

5. Pet Parade

It's only fair that our furry (or feathered) family members should have a tree of their own this Christmas! In honor of your animal companions, this theme is loaded with fun reminders that Christmas is really going to the dogs . . .

Top 5 Elements:

- Pet treat-shaped ornaments: dog bones, catnip balls, faux treats
- Pictures of your pets in cute frames
- Animal-themed ornaments including figurines, painted discs, and balls
- A metal tub with "Dinner" painted on to serve as fun "dog-bowl" base
- Ribbon featuring paw prints or an animal-printed motif

6. Touched by an Angel

Elegant touches of ivory, gold, and cream accent a tree loaded with sparkling gems, feather-soft accents, and lots of twinkling light to create a tree that is soft and romantic. A perfect look for a bedroom, formal living room, or entry.

Top 5 Elements:

- Blown glass and cut crystal ornaments in gold, ivory, and mercury glass
- Ivory, cream, or gold brushed flower stems such as magnolia or poinsettia
- Angels, crosses, churches, and wings in neutral hues
- Strands of twinkle lights to weave into the branches
- Wide ribbon in metallic gold or ivory

7. Starry Nights

If you are looking for an elegant and festive look that will carry you from Christmas all the way through New Year's Eve, then this theme is a perfect choice. Deep blues, reflective silvers, and metallic golds sparkle right on through the holiday season. This theme does best on a lighter-colored tree such as a flocked, frosted, or tinsel.

Top 5 Elements:

- Assorted ornaments in shades of blue including extradeep midnight blues
- Various stars and burst-shaped ornaments in silver, champagne, and gold
- Rich ribbon in a sparkly midnight blue

- Extra strands of twinkle lights to weave into the tree for maximum sparkle
- A lighted star topper for the top of the tree

8. Holiday Garden

If you are a gardener, a flower lover, or just like a little touch of spring in the darkness of winter, then this theme is sure to make your heart happy. Loaded full of blossoms, birds, and butterflies, this look will transport you straight to your favorite garden spot in the middle of December! Perfect on any style of green tree.

Top 5 Elements:

- A collection of flower stems in pastel hues (hydrangeas, peonies, lilies, etc.)
- Blown-glass ornaments in butterflies, flowers, bees, birds, and bugs
- Ribbon printed in florals or solid ribbon in hues pulled from the flowers
- A full tree bouquet for the topper of the tree
- Nests, branches, and other organic elements to tuck into the tree

9. 50s Vintage

There was perhaps no generation that influenced the look and style of our modern-day Christmas more than the 1950s. This throwback tree will have you feeling nostalgic for all of the right reasons! Perfect for a shiny tinsel tree or a classic tree with big-bulb lights.

Top 5 Elements:

- Reflector ornaments
- Vintage-style lights (big, round bulbs; bubble candles; or multicolored)
- Classic Santa-, reindeer-, snowman-styled ornaments
- Glass-ball garlands or tinsel-trimmed garland
- Shiny string tinsel for dropping on as the final element

10. Christmas at the Cabin

Let nature be your muse with this warm and rustic-inspired theme. Wooden carvings, grapevine balls, and feather picks bring the outdoors in. This theme looks best on a natural pine or fir tree but can be carried off on a frosted or flocked tree as well.

Top 5 Elements:

- Carved wooden figurines, painted wooden disc ornaments, and wood balls
- Feather picks and feather-covered ball ornaments
- Grapevine balls and large pinecones to nestle into the branches
- Sticks, branches, and pine stems to add extra texture and interest
- Reflective glass ornaments in ambers, browns, and shades of green

11. Bears and Friends

A fun and kitschy theme reminiscent of childhood camping trips. Red-and-black-checked gingham adds folksy flair while woodland creatures add a fun touch. Perfect for a little boy's room or a family den space.

Top 5 Elements:

- Red-and-black-checked gingham/flannel ribbon to weave in and out of the tree.
- Woodland creature ornaments in faux fur such as bears, deer, racoons, and owls
- Miniature wooden skis, lanterns, cabins, and other rustic elements
- Faux popcorn or red berry garlands
- Large cross-country or downhill skis to wire into the tree for a focal point

12. Victorian Traditions

The Victorian Era heralded in the celebration of Christmas Day for all people, so it is only fitting to decorate a tree worthy of such a rich heritage. Victorian Christmas trees were often elaborate affairs featuring real fruit, candies, and candles. The spirit of Christmas is alive and well in this historically themed tree.

Top 5 Elements:

- Paper nosegays filled with small bouquets of dried or silk flowers
- Foil-wrapped faux fruit ornaments including apples, oranges, and pomegranates
- Battery-powered clip-on candles for the tips of the branches
- Small beaded garlands to layer all over the branches
- Cardboard cutout ornaments featuring prints of Victorian-era Holiday scenes

13. O Holy Night

Let your hearts and tree keep the true reason for the season front and center with this Nativity-themed tree. The soft shades of blue, green, and gray keep this look current and updated. If you have an actual Nativity set tucked away in your decorations, be sure to display it prominently near the tree for maximum impact!

Top 5 Elements:

- Ball ornaments in soft blues, greens, and grays
- Nativity ornaments painted on balls, cut out of wood, and carved in ceramic
- Star of David-shaped star ornaments in different sizes
- Velvet or flocked ribbon in one of the featured colors
- Scripture verses hand-lettered on disc or ball ornaments

14. Country Christmas

Christmas in the country calls for simple decorations, a limited color palette, and classic combinations. Red and white form the base of this theme that fits perfectly on a tree cut fresh from the farm. (Or an artificial tree that looks like it at least!)

Top 5 Elements:

- Red-and-white ticking-striped ribbon for tying simple bows
- A galvanized metal washtub or wooden bucket to serve as a base
- Chalkboard ornaments handwritten with favorite holiday quotes
- Cotton, berry, or holly picks for tucking randomly into the branches
- Tin, ceramic, wood, and other "farmhouse" textured ornaments

15. Llama Days

Llamas are fuzzy, fun, and fabulous for your Christmas tree theme! Think outside of the box with this look by incorporating bright colors, unexpected motifs, and of course, lots of llamas! Perfect for a colorful table-top or slim-lined tree.

Top 5 Elements:

- Llama ornaments featuring painted balls, figurines, and stuffed llamas
- Bright and shiny balls in shades of red, pink, lime green, and orange
- Printed banner garlands in bright colors and fun prints

- Pom-pom picks or shiny ball picks
- Cactus, succulent, and/or Mexican flower stems for tucking into the tree

16. Plaid Tidings

An updated take on a traditional Christmas tree theme. Create a sense of unity and harmony with all of your mismatched ornaments collected through the years by adding in accents of Holiday plaid and touches of red. Looks best on a traditional green tree.

Top 5 Elements:

- Strands of colored lights to add into the tree (if using a clear-lit tree)
- Collection of mismatched ornaments gathered through the years
- 3"–4" plaid ribbon in reds, greens, whites, and possibly blues
- Several stems of a large red flower or berry spray (poinsettia, magnolia, etc.)
- Sets of coordinated red blown-glass ornaments to tie everything together

17. Baking Days

If the holidays mean hours upon hours spent baking sweet treats in the kitchen, then this might be the tree for you! Red, white, and turquoise fill a tree laden with gingerbread, cookies, and cakes. Toss in a few baking tools for good measure, and you'll have a tree that looks good enough to eat!

Top 5 Elements:

- Gingerbread cookie, decorated cake, iced cookie, cinnamon roll ornaments
- Rolling pin, mixing bowl, cookie cutters, and/or whisk ornaments
- Picks featuring cupcakes, gingerbread accents, or marshmallows
- Red-and-white accented ribbon
- Ornaments in reds, whites, and accents of turquoise

18. Silver and Gold

Timeless and classic are two words that can be used to describe this tree theme. The use of mixed metallics has the magic of looking both vintage and completely modern at the exact same time. Adding in accents of sparkly champagne and crystal pieces keeps this tree theme shining as the star it was meant to be! This look is lovely on both green- and white-based trees.

Top 5 Elements:

- A collection of silver, gold, champagne, and mercury glass ornaments
- Crystal icicles, chandelier-style drop ornaments, and tear drops
- Delicate crystal or silver and gold ball garlands
- Silver or gold flowers dipped in glitter or frosted with crystal accents
- Elaborate ribbon in golds, silvers, and champagnes

19. Red Birds and Berries

This is the perfect theme for refreshing a traditionally themed tree without having to start from scratch. Red, green, and white ornaments are brought to life with accents of red cardinals and berry branches. This look is especially gorgeous on a white, flocked tree.

Top 5 Elements:

- Red, green, and white glass or ceramic ornaments
- Branches featuring holly and red berries
- Cardinal clips, ornaments, or figurines
- Wired plaid or red satin ribbon
- A collection of family favorite ornaments to incorporate into the branches

20. Red-and-Green Christmas

Traditions are celebrated at Christmas, and the traditional colors of red and green will never go out of style during the Holidays. Keep this combo fresh and current with the addition of cut-glass ornaments, fabulous ribbon, and some show-stopping florals. A classic green tree is all you need for this timeless look!

Top 5 Elements:

- A combination of red-and-green cut-glass ornaments
- 4"-wide ribbon in a beautiful red-and-green print or plaid
- Large scaled flowers (poinsettias, magnolias, or amaryllis are good choices)
- Blown-glass ornaments in traditional styles (Santas, trees, stars, etc.)
- Delicate beaded or glass garlands in red, green, and possibly gold

21. Santa's Workshop

Christmas is a time for children, and what better way to celebrate the magic of the season than with a tree dedicated to Santa and his workshop! Toys, tools, and mischievous elves are sure to bring a smile to the faces of children of all ages.

Top 5 Elements:

- Wooden tool ornaments such as hammers, drills, and saws
- Old-fashioned toys and/or toy ornaments like dolls, cars, and jack-in-the-boxes
- Elf figurines wired to look like they are climbing the tree or holding the toys
- Classic Santa figurine styled ornaments
- Ribbon featuring Santa's buckle or printed with "Ho-Ho-Ho"

22. Snowman Fun

Frosty and his frozen friends are the stars of this snow-covered tree theme! Perfect for anyone looking for a tree that can be left out for the entire winter season. This theme looks best on a flocked or frosted tree of course!

Top 5 Elements:

- Cotton-wrapped faux-snowball ornaments
- Snowman figurines, painted ornaments, and stuffed ornaments
- Snowball or cotton ball garlands
- Woven mittens and miniature sweater ornaments
- A black top hat for the topper on the tree

23. Holly-Days

The inspiration for this simple tree comes from the classic evergreen favorite: holly. Holly comes in many different varieties, but for this look we are looking for the more delicately shaped leaves featuring those of white and green with bright red berries. This is the perfect theme for a simple, yet showy green or flocked tree.

Top 5 Elements:

- Several stems of holly with red berries and green-and-white variegated leaves
- White ribbon with printed or woven holly accents
- Bright-red and crisp-white ornaments in different shapes (ball, drop, finial, etc.)

- Red or white glass (or plastic) ball garland
- Small spun-glass icicles to hang all over the very tips of the tree branches

24. Home for the Holidays

If your travels take you far and wide, then have fun showing off all of your favorite destinations on a travel-themed tree. Postcards from the various cities you've visited can be glued to cardboard and hung on the tree for inexpensive ornaments, and an open suitcase filled with packages carries your theme all the way down to the base.

Top 5 Elements:

- Ornaments picked up from your travels or featuring popular tourist destinations
- World globe ornaments and/or map ornaments
- Banners featuring flags from various countries to serve as a garland
- Postcards from your travels placed in small frames or tied on with ribbon
- A big "Home for the Holidays" sign wired into the front of the tree

25. A French Holiday

Have you ever dreamed of spending Christmas sipping champagne under the Eiffel Tower? Then why not bring a Parisian Christmas straight to your living room this year? Sparkling silvers, elegant golds, and the faintest of blues will transport you to the romantic streets of the City of Love during the Holidays. This look is lovely on a white, tinsel, or flocked tree.

Top 5 Elements:

- Mercury glass ornaments in silvers, golds, and light French blue.
- Crystal or beaded glass garlands for cascading off of the branches
- Eiffel Tower and fleur-de-lis ornaments in silvers and golds
- Wide ribbon in shiny silver or pale blue
- Chandelier or crystal drop ornaments to add sparkle and shine

26. Citrus Delight

Does the thought of another red-and-green Christmas tree have you wanting to spit out your eggnog? Then this refreshingly cool tree might be for you! Embracing the fresh, crisp colors of the in-season tangerines, lemons, limes, and grapefruits will liven up your tree in no time flat! A light-green tree can be harder to find but creates a perfect backdrop for this unexpected theme.

Top 5 Elements:

- Satin ribbon in shades of coral, yellow, and lime green
- Jeweled orange, lemon, lime, and pineapple ornaments
- Branches of lemons and limes
- Disk ornaments painted in garden topiaries, butterflies, and flowers
- Ball ornaments in citrus hues to carry the colors throughout the tree

27. "Fan"-Tastic Tree

A true sports fan would be remiss if his tree didn't support his favorite team in one way or another, so why not have an entire tree dedicated to your favorite team (or teams)?! This tree theme is perfect for a tabletop or slim tree in a man cave, boy's room, or family den.

Top 5 Elements:

- Ornaments featuring the team's gear (footballs, soccer balls, basketballs, etc.)
- Ribbon or banners in team colors
- Ornaments in the team's colors, printed with the name or featuring star players
- Glass ornaments of "Fan Favorite" food such as hotdogs, nachos, popcorn, etc.
- In place of a traditional tree skirt, use a team-printed blanket or throw

28. Feathered Friends

The holidays are the perfect time to celebrate with friends of all types including our feathered ones! Feather accents, colorful bird ornaments, and natural nests tucked into the branches result in a creative and colorful design. Looks best on a natural, green tree.

Top 5 Elements:

- Clip-on and hanging bird ornaments in glass, ceramic, and faux feathers
- Feather picks for tucking into the tree
- Nests to be laid in the branches
- Sticks with small nests and birds glued on for the topper of the tree
- Colorful blown-glass balls in colors pulled from the bird ornaments

29. Southern Comfort

Christmas in the deep south is a festive affair where the crystal comes out and the good silver is polished and ready for lots of use. The warmer weather means that Southern homes at Christmas are usually lighter, fresher, and less "frosted" than their snow-buried Northern neighbors. Traditional reds are paired with Chinese blues to create a look that is crisp, clean, and quintessentially Southern.

Top 5 Elements:

- Red and blue velvet ribbon
- Red ball ornaments
- Blue chinoiserie vase, urn, and ball ornaments
- Bundles of faux red roses
- White magnolia flower sprays

30. Noah's Ark

Loads of different animals in pairs make up this fun and quirky tree. Small boat ornaments and lots of blue balls are reminiscent of the ark and all of that rain! Perfect on a smaller tree for a nursery or young child's room.

Top 5 Elements:

- Pairs of animal ornaments (lions, elephants, tigers, monkeys, etc.)
- Blown-glass ark or large boat ornaments
- Glass balls in various sizes and shades of blue
- Icicles that taper into a drop (similar to rain drops)
- Blue satin ribbon

31. Crafted Creations

Let your handiworks take center stage on this craft-inspired tree. This is a fun and affordable tree to decorate with children or for a kid's room or playroom. The look is meant to be fun, creative, and colorful, so have fun and embrace the imperfections! Perfect for a tabletop or potted small tree.

Top 5 Elements:

- Handmade paper chain garlands
- Clay stars, balls, and/or other favorite shapes
- Paper angels, glittered stars, or painted trees

- Decorated glass or plastic ball ornaments
- Pipe cleaner ornaments

32. Glad Tide-ings

If you're celebrating the season with sand instead of snow, then a beach-themed tree is perfect! We're going to leave the pink flamingo and flip-flop ornaments to the tourists and decorate this tree with the soft colors of sea glass and the tide as our inspiration. Looks lovely on a sandy white tree or a softer green tree.

Top 5 Elements:

- Glass balls in sea glass shades of blue, green, and frosted clear
- Sea grass stems for the topper
- Natural shells, faux sand dollar, and starfish ornaments
- Pieces of netting to weave into the tree in place of a garland
- Driftwood branches to wire into the tree

33. Rockin' around the Christmas Tree

Kick off the holidays with a rock-and-roll inspired tree that can carry you from Christmas all the way through the New Year. Jazzy reds, blacks, and silvers create a modern look that is accented with mirrored ornaments and shiny disco balls. Looks sharp on a silver tinsel or white tree.

Top 5 Elements:

- Shiny red and silver ornaments in various shapes and sizes
- Black and silver music notes
- Silver foiled/shiny ribbon
- Mirrored stars, instruments, or miniature disco balls
- Guitar, drums, and saxophone ornaments

34. Cozy Christmas

If all of the hustle and bustle of the holidays has you wanting nothing more than to snuggle up under a big, comfy blanket with a steaming mug of hot cocoa, then you have found your theme! A neutral palette of whites, creams, and grays is calming to the senses, while all of the cozy and soft textures will calm your frazzled nerves. Use a fluffy blanket as a tree skirt, and you'll complete this look with perfection.

Top 5 Elements:

- Yarn ball ornaments in white, creams, and grays
- Felted wool sweater, mitten, and sock ornaments
- Natural wood and ivory ceramic ornaments
- Knitted, crocheted, or felted garlands
- Frosted or natural pinecones to nestle in the branches

35. The "Man Tree"

The final tree on our list of themes is dedicated to the men. While most trees are loaded down with glitz and sparkle, on this tree you are more likely to spot a fishing lure than you are a glittered ball. While recommended decor items will be listed below, feel free to cater this design to the hobbies and pursuits of the men in your home. Looks best on a traditional green tree.

Top 5 Elements:

- Ornaments with fishing poles, decorative lures, minishotguns, and/or golf clubs
- Large pinecones to tuck in the branches
- Strands of solid green or brown lights to brighten look
- Branches with lures tied to the tips to serve as a topper
- "Man Cave" printed signs, camouflage printed balls, hot rod/car ornaments

Hopefully this list of thirty-five tree themes will get your creative juices flowing when it comes to designing a new tree or updating an existing tree. If you are one of the many households that has a family tree featuring a collection of ornaments gathered throughout the years, consider adding a smaller themed tree in a bedroom, kitchen, or den space. Some of my clients even have a different themed tree in every room of their house, including bathrooms! No matter how big or small your home, there is always room for a Christmas tree of some type, so have fun brainstorming and then get to decorating!

Bonus | Putting It All Away

If you cannot tell by now, I love Christmas! I will happily decorate from July (when we usually put our first tree up in the store) into late December without complaint. However, I do not, and I repeat, do not like to pack up Christmas decorations! I (somewhat) jokingly tell clients that I charge three times more to come and pack up their decor than I do to put it up. Luckily very few clients take me up on that offer!

While I do not enjoy packing up the holiday decorations, it is a chore that must be done and, if done right, can save you time, energy, and headaches in the next year. There is nothing more frustrating than opening up boxes with broken ornaments or tangled lights from the previous year. Properly stored decorations will last you for years to come.

One tip that I have learned from working with repeat clients year after year is to always take pictures of the decorations and tree before you pack them up at the end of the season. It is also helpful to make notes on what you loved, what you want to keep working on, and anything that you will need to add or replace next season. You might think that you will remember exactly how you placed that ribbon, or how the topper looked, but more than likely you will not!

Through the years, I have learned to take pictures and either save them in a folder on a phone or computer marked Christmas Decor, or I print them off and place them in the totes with the decorations. That way when you are ready to decorate next year, you will be able to remember exactly what you did that you want to replicate and what needed to be done differently in the new season.

Sanity Saver: Photos are a decorator's best friend. Taking great shots of your tree allows you to remember what you wanted to update and change, while also helping you to recreate the parts that you love and want to keep the same.

Now that you have documented your tree design and made notes as to what worked, what did not, and what you need to purchase or replace for the next season, it is time to take everything off the tree and store it away safe and sound. I recommend taking the items off of the tree in reverse order of how you placed them on the tree so that they will all be together when you get ready to decorate next year.

If you have space, there are tree bags on the market that allow you to cover your entire tree, decorations and all, and simply roll it into a closet or garage for the next year! If you don't have a room dedicated only to Christmas tree storage, though (I have one client who had her home custom built with a Christmas tree-sized closet so she never has to redecorate her tree!), you will need to undecorate your tree and store the individual pieces.

HERE ARE SOME TIPS FOR STORING EACH ITEM:

* THE TREE: Remember to store your tree in a temperature controlled space with minimal moisture. If you are talented enough to get your tree back in its original box, that is a suitable container. You may also purchase tree bags with handles and wheels to make storing your tree even easier.

* THE LIGHTS: If you use a real tree, or add additional lights to your artificial tree, be sure to store your lights in a temperature-controlled space with minimal moisture. I recommend wrapping your lights around an empty wrapping tube or paper towel tube to keep them from getting tangled into a big mess! Make sure you wrap your lights so the male end (the side with the prongs) is at the front of the roll in order to be able to plug in and go the next season.

* GARLANDS, WRAPPED RIBBON, OR MESH: For your garlands and mesh I recommend purchasing the extralong plastic totes and laying them in layers as flat as possible.

For your wired ribbon, wrap it around an empty cardboard tube to keep it looking as good as new for the next year.

❄ TREE BOUQUETS, CENTER POINTS, AND BOWS: Plastic totes are the best bet for your tree bouquets, center points, and bows as well. I recommend purchasing enough totes so that you do not have to crowd your pieces. Placing rolled-up balls of tissue paper in the loops of your bows will hold their shape for the next season.

❄ ORNAMENTS: I love the new divided boxes and totes that are on the market for ornaments! These containers keep your fragile ornaments from bumping, but I still recommend wrapping your more delicate items in tissue paper or bubble wrap for added insulation. If your ornaments came packaged in nice boxes, you can repackage them and pack the individual boxes together in a larger tote. Do not overload your boxes or the weight of the pieces can crush the ornaments on the bottom.

❄ TREE TOPPERS AND TOPPER BOWS: Tree toppers are best stored alone in a single tote, or stored upright in a large container with a plastic bag wrapped over the top. Tree topper bows stay very nice if they are hung on a hanger and covered with a large bag. Dry cleaner bags work perfectly for this. Stuffing the loops with tissue and rolling up the long tails will keep them looking their best for the next season.

Any other pieces such as your fillers or base decor pieces can be wrapped in tissue paper and layered in a tote with the heavier items on the bottom.

You have now completed Christmas Tree Decorating 101 and hopefully have gained the knowledge and skills needed to design a tree you will enjoy for years to come. As I wrap up this step-by-step guide to decorating your tree, I want to say thank you for giving me the opportunity to share in the making of many special memories. The Christmas tree is the center of so many special times, and I hope this book gives you the knowledge and skills needed to design a tree that brings you joy and enjoyment for many years!

Blessings and Many Celebrations!

Cassie Kitzmiller

Custom Christmas Tree-Decorating Checklist

I f you are new to tree decorating, or if you are working on an entirely new tree style or theme, it can be overwhelming to think about all of the different elements needed for a tree. It can also be very confusing to try to figure out in your head how many of each item to get to complete your look.

The checklist to follow will serve as a guide, helping you figure out what you need to purchase to create your best-looking tree ever. Simply fill in the blanks and when you are finished, you will have a personalized tree-decorating guide just for you!

I have included a basic checklist below with the questions and information needed to create a beautiful tree, but if you would like a template that you can download and fill in on your phone/computer or print and take with you, simply go to the following site: www.finding-beautyintheeveryday.com/checklist.

Once you are there, supply in your email address and a beautifully designed Checklist will arrive in your inbox!

CHRISTMAS TREE CHECKLIST

Tree Style or Theme:

Tree Type and Size:

- [ ] Real or Artificial?
- [ ]
- [ ]
- [ ]

Lighting: (15' per 1' of tree)

- [ ] Type and Amount:
- [ ]
- [ ]
- [ ]

Garlands, Mesh or Wrapped Ribbon: Type and Amount

- [ ] 8-10 6' garlands for a 7½' tree. 20 yards of ribbon for a 7' tree and 100' of Mesh for 7½' tree.
- [ ]
- [ ]
- [ ]
- [ ]

Tree Diamond: Items Used and Number or Each-

10–12 items to cover ¾ of 7½' tree. 14–16 for full.

Focal Points:

Number and Item:

Ornaments: Shapes/Sizes

Number of Each:

Finishing Touches:

Items and Number:

Coordinating Base:

Look and Items:

Custom Topper: Height, Fillers, and Centerpoint-

Item and Number Needed of Each:

Words from the Author

Thank you for joining me on this journey into the art of learning to decorate a beautiful Christmas tree! While there is absolutely no "wrong" way to decorate a tree, I hope this book inspires you to look at your tree in a new way and try some new tricks this year.

Even though I am an interior designer by trade, I have three young boys in my household, so you had better believe my own tree is far from "perfect." There are always more ornaments on the bottom (where small hands can reach) than the top, Spiderman and Mickey Mouse are more commonly used than elegant glass balls, and there is not a flower in sight, but our tree represents my family and our story and I love it. So in closing I would like to remind you that a truly beautiful tree is more about the love around its base than the decorations on its branches.

And as always, Celebrate Abundantly!

Festively Yours,

Cassie Kitzmiller

Acknowledgments

Photography provided by Raz Imports, Christy Harris Photography, and Cassie Kitzmiller.

This book would not have been possible if not for the guidance and direction of many special people:

KELLY THOMAS: You set the love of Christmas in my heart as a young child and supported me down the path to following my heart and not only my head.

TIM THOMAS: You have believed in me and encouraged me since I was your little pumpkin. Thank you for your love and leadership through the years.

RACHEL MCCRACKEN: You are an example of friendship at its finest. This book is better because you were a part of it!

MARTY GLASGOW: Fearless mentor, friend, and business partner. I would not be who I am, nor have the experience I do, if not for you taking a chance on a young college student over ten years ago. Thank you.

MY LAUNCH TEAM: It takes a village to raise a child (or a book), and you all have been my village! Thank you from the bottom of my heart for your insight, guidance, and support of this book from conception through publishing.

TO MY CLIENTS AND CLASS LADIES: Thank you for opening your homes and hearts by allowing me to decorate your homes and teach you all I know about the holidays! Your projects and trees have inspired me and challenged me to become a better designer and Christmas elf through the years.

SELF-PUBLISHING SCHOOL CREATORS AND FELLOW AUTHORS: This book would not have been possible without your guidance, insights, and advice throughout this entire process.

If you are interested in learning about the process of writing, launching, and publishing your own book, type in the link below for an informative introductory video!

https://xe172.isrefer.com/go/curcust/bookbrosinc5208

Product Shopping Directory

Through my years in the design industry I have had the privilege of working with many wonderful companies that offer amazing products. Here is a list of some of my favorite Companies and Products that I turn to when stocking my stores or purchasing merchandise for my clients.

   Companies with an * next to their names have compensated me for mentioning their products in this book. This allows me to keep production costs down and provides the opportunity to offer this book at a lower sales price. I only recommend products that I have personally tried or have been recommended to me by friends and clients.

*THE MAGIC WAND LIGHT COMPANY

As discussed in the "Lighting Your Tree" chapter. A magical solution to turning on and off your tree lights with ease: Come in Your Choice of Three Colors.

https://magiclightwand.com

*NOELLE SEASONAL DÉCOR AND GIFTS GALORE!

My flagship Seasonal and Gift Store!! A fun and festive holiday and gift store located in downtown Jonesborough, TN.

https://www.facebook.com/Noelle123
https://www.instagram.com/NoelleDecor
1-423-913-8000

Call for availability and shipping info on Bedrock Tree Farm Candles, Magic Light Wands, Raz Lighting and Décor, and many of the other items mentioned.

123 E. Main St. Jonesborough, TN 37659

RAZ IMPORTS

The King of the Christmas product empire and my go-to source for specialty lighting, ornaments, tabletop decor, flowers, picks, and garlands. They do not sell directly to the public, but their products can be found in specialty stores across the United States, including *Noelle Seasonal Décor and Gifts Galore!*

https://www.razimports.com

STARRY TREASURES

The talented creators of the lighted Moravian Star toppers, ornaments, and overhead lights mentioned in the "Tree Topper" chapter.

http://starrytreasures.com

BEDROCK TREE FARMS

Real tree farm located in Rhode Island and inventor of the most realistic-smelling fir tree candles ever. They do not sell directly to the public, but there is a list of retailers on their website including *Noelle Seasonal Décor and Gifts Galore.*

http://bedrocktreefarm.com

About the Author

Cassie is an undercover elf, Licensed Interior Designer, mother to three energetic boys, and an avid Christmas lover. With over ten years of Interior Design experience, Cassie loves to share her skills and expertise with others to help them make their own homes beautiful all year long. This is Cassie's first book in the "Celebrate Abundantly" series and she plans to provide her readers with more books featuring Designer Tips and Techniques to utilize throughout their Holiday homes.

To see more about what is to come in the "Celebrate Abundantly" series and for more holiday tips, check out her website at findingbeautyintheeveryday.com or send her an email at authorcassiekitzmiller@gmail.com.

Wish List

....

....

....

....

....

....

....

....

....

....

....

Wish List

Wish List

Wish List

....

....

....

....

....

....

....

....

....

....

....

....